Julia McGuinness is a freelance
She writes for Redemptorist's '
Times, and has produced article
counsellor, she works both privately and at a National Health
Service general practitioners' surgery. Julia is also a qualified
Myers-Briggs consultant and has run workshops in secular
environments and church settings. She is a Reader at St Thomas'
and All Saints', Ellesmere Port with St Lawrence's, Stoak Village,
a parish with a varied range of churchmanship across its different services.

CREATIVE PRAYING
IN GROUPS

Julia McGuinness

First published in Great Britain in 2005

Society for Promoting Christian Knowledge
36 Causton Street
London SW1P 4ST

The author and publisher have made every effort to ensure that the
external website and email addresses included in this book are correct and
up to date at the time of going to press. The author and publisher are not
responsible for the content, quality or continuing accessibility of the sites.

Scripture quotations are from the New Revised Standard Version of the
Bible, copyright © 1989 by the Division of Christian Education of the
National Council of the Churches of Christ in the USA. Used by
permission. All rights reserved.

British Library Cataloguing-in-Publication Data
A catalogue record for this book is available from the British Library

ISBN 0–281–05733–8

1 3 5 7 9 10 8 6 4 2

Typeset by Graphicraft Ltd., Hong Kong
Printed in Great Britain by Book Marque Ltd

Contents

Part 1
THREADING PRAYER THROUGH
THE MEETING

Part 2
WEAVING PRAYER THROUGH
THE YEAR

Contents

Acknowledgements

I'd like to thank my husband Gordon, whose enthusiasm for exploring new ideas and suggesting different approaches has made him a valuable sounding board and source of inspiration when my own energy has been running low.

I'm also grateful to St Barnabas' Church in Inham Nook: their warm hearts and open spirits enabled us all to learn so much about the rich experience of Christian worship during the time we shared together.

Finally, I wish to thank those in St Thomas' and All Saints' in Ellesmere Port whose personal encouragement and practical support have helped this book into being. Most particularly, I'm indebted to Linda Tudor for the creative insights and research skills she has contributed to the development of these ideas.

General introduction

———◆◆◆———

Preface

Small groups past and present

After the big celebration in the marquee at the Christian conference, or the lively bustle of church on Sunday, we may find a mid-week meeting with a handful of people something of an anticlimax. Yet small groups have been the bedrock and the lifeblood of the Christian Church from the beginning.

Jesus started his ministry by choosing twelve disciples: a group large enough to reflect a diversity of backgrounds and experience – from collecting taxes to catching fish – but small enough to offer space for personal attention and participation. The disciples learnt by what Jesus did as well as what he said, alongside the challenge of sharing a common life.

This pattern of community continued. The book of Acts demonstrates the centrality of small groups to early church life. Paul's letters include greetings to the church in the home of Priscilla and Aquila, among others. In an era before church buildings, and in a pagan society with the gospel at the margins, the home was the obvious place for believers to meet.

God used these humble gatherings to establish the Church across the Roman Empire, and small groups have played a strategic part in nearly every renewal movement since; their importance has been recognized by Christian pioneers from

Francis of Assisi to John Wesley. We're often tempted to measure spiritual significance by numbers alone, but in God's Kingdom a group's size does not limit the resources available for fruitful Christian growth.

At a time when Christians can feel isolated in the world and anonymous in the church, the small group is as relevant as ever. It offers comfort, support and challenge. In this personal setting we are known by name, and our presence – and absence – is noticed. We can develop deeper relationships with one another; receive and give encouragement; share, explore, support and worship. We find a safe place to express our real faith, warts and all, and help in nurturing it to maturity.

A vital element in this growth process is coming to Christ together in prayer. As Christ taught his own small group of disciples to pray, he declared, '*When* you pray,' not, '*If* you pray' (Luke 11.2).

Praying together: power point or pressure point?

Small group prayer can be a significant spiritual power point, yet we may experience it as a pressure point.

As leaders we may feel our resources are limited. We know the small group cannot offer the uplifting musical support of the larger-scale Sunday service. We may also sense our personal limitations; perhaps we feel neither sufficiently seasoned prayer warriors nor expert enough theologians to lead others in prayer.

A group's reservations can emerge in how prayer gets squeezed out of a meeting for lack of time. Most of us would rather avoid the embarrassing silence that can descend when the group is asked to volunteer 'items for prayer'. At the opposite extreme, we can allow the sharing of prayer needs to extend into a discussion that eats up nearly all the actual prayer time. This can mean hurriedly finishing a meeting with a few mumbled prayer requests or one all-embracing, eloquent prayer from the most spiritually outgoing group member.

Prayer in a small group presents a particular challenge. We're neither behind closed doors in our own private devotions, nor simply silently affirming those leading intercessions in a church service. We may feel a greater pressure to participate, plus a higher potential embarrassment factor if we do take the plunge, pray out loud and muddle our words.

But handled sensitively, a group offers a great opportunity to learn to pray together. The leader's approach is vital: prayer is an expression of relationship, not a test of our spiritual credentials. If prayer is linked to achievement, then the stakes for 'success' are high. If we see it as part of our growing relationship with the Lord, then prayer becomes an activity where we can learn, without always having to get it right. We don't need to have arrived; just to be on the journey together.

Where the leader can foster an atmosphere of mutual acceptance, a common purpose and loving support in the group in general, this will spill over into the group's prayer in particular. It will become easier to explore, experiment, and move out of our comfort zones.

Prayer is best approached in a manner that is relaxed without being casual, where people are invited to respond, not pushed to participate, and where we make space for all to contribute.

The tapestry of prayer

Prayer, like a tapestry, has many different threads.

Companionship

The heart of our Christian faith is coming to know the one who has created us, redeemed us and called us to be his own people.

It's hardly surprising that God desires a relationship with those made in his image. In the Trinity we glimpse a picture of divine companionship expressed through prayer: Jesus in his earthly life constantly prayed to the Father, who sent his Holy Spirit in response. It's the Spirit's activity that enables *us* to respond to God's invitation to enfold us within the loving companionship of the Trinity. When we have a desire to pray, we're saying yes to an initiative God has already taken as his Spirit prompts our hearts. The Spirit also equips us by helping us find ways and means of expressing ourselves in prayer. So we are not on our own.

Communication

Personal relationships depend on communication to survive and thrive. This can happen through words, whether formal or conversational, animated or reflective, fluent or halting. Sometimes we want to choose our words more carefully, so we write them down, perhaps in a letter or speech. At other times we struggle to find our own words to convey what we want to say, so we look beyond ourselves, using words others have written to suit the occasion – in a greeting card or poem, for example.

Words can also help us communicate with God, from spontaneous utterances to prayers written by ourselves or others, and just as we declare words in unison to express shared sentiments in ordinary life – from a wedding toast to a football chant – so we can express our united Christian message by speaking the words of liturgical prayers together. Such spiritual unity is often summed up in a single word shared at the end of a prayer: 'Amen', meaning, 'So be it' or 'We agree'.

But words are only one element in our relating to one another. Research indicates that over 90 per cent of face-to-face communication happens via such means as tone of voice, facial expression and body language. What implication does this have for those inhibited in group prayer, because they find it hard to express themselves in words?

Communication between God and his creation goes way beyond words. The Spirit, Paul tells us, 'intercedes with sighs too deep for words' (Romans 8.26); God is an artist, whose 'eternal power and divine nature', though invisible, 'have been understood and seen through the things he has made' (Romans 1.20); Jeremiah was told to 'go down to the potter's house', to receive a prophetic word underlined by a powerful visual aid (Jeremiah 18); the Lord gave Peter a dramatic vision of unclean animals as acceptable food to overturn Peter's understanding that the gospel was for Jews alone (Acts 10.9–15). The very life of Jesus is a communication of God's character, love and power. Through Jesus' relationships, his miracles and ministry, death and resurrection, God makes himself known to humankind.

Moreover, Jesus communicated beyond words: he shed tears at Lazarus' tomb (John 11.35), and healed by spreading mud over a blind man's eyes and instructing him to wash in the Siloam pool (John 9.6).

As we worship God with our whole selves, action, body language and posture are powerful communicators. Mary anointed Jesus' feet with perfume as he dined (John 12.3); Peter fell down before Jesus in worship (Luke 5.8); Jairus fell at Jesus' feet to beg for his daughter's healing (Luke 8.41); Paul tells Timothy that believers should 'lift up holy hands' in worship (1 Timothy 2.8), rather than raising angry fists in argument.

Music also releases communication from the places words cannot reach. Psalm 150 exhorts us to praise God with trumpets and tambourines, plus any other instrument we can lay our hands on! Paul encourages believers to worship in song, 'making melody to the Lord in your hearts' (Ephesians 5.19).

Communion

Have you ever been with someone who's talked a great deal, yet left you feeling nothing has been communicated? Or shared a deep silence with a loved one that has been intimate and meaningful? Sometimes we're anxious to fill every available space with noise or activity, yet when God visited Elijah, his presence came in 'sheer silence', not the drama of earthquake, wind and fire (1 Kings 19.12).

In worship we move from communicating to communing with God himself. Communion is the deepest of connections – when we know ourselves to be at one with our Lord, drawn into his very presence. This happens for some in corporate worship, as they sense themselves lifted above everyday concerns; for others, it is in stillness, as they tune into an awareness of God's Spirit deep within.

Prayer times that make space for people to commune with Christ demand discipline to arrange. We're used to thinking of prayer as something we do, rather than as someone we receive, but with such prayer, the leader is no longer under pressure to create an activity that 'works'. The challenge is to set things up and step back, trusting that God wants to make himself known to his people. As one wise Christian leader said: 'If you make space, then people will connect with God on their own.'

Small groups and prayer: the canvas and the weavers

If prayer is like a tapestry of different strands, the small group setting and members form its canvas and weavers.

Group type

Small groups in church life are many and varied. At one end of the spectrum are home groups, fellowship groups, and cell groups. While they may fit into the wider church body in different ways, such groups generally meet with ongoing regularity and have a fairly stable membership and a wide-ranging agenda of learning, sharing and mutual support, worship and evangelism.

Other groups may have a more limited shelf life: a confirmation class or ecumenical Lent group, for example. Such groups may include those who do not know one another outside the meeting, and have come together primarily to learn or follow a particular course with a designated ending.

Your small group's clientele may be a wide mixture of folk, or represent one area of church life, such as a Young Mums' Bible study, or a particular age group, as in a Youth Fellowship. How might these factors affect praying together?

Group size

Received wisdom indicates that the optimal number for an effective small group lies somewhere between eight and twelve, though Jesus' promise that 'where two or three are gathered in my name, I am there among them' (Matthew 18.20) assures us he'll be there whatever the turnout. Nevertheless, group size may affect *how* you pray together. Where numbers are very low, people can feel vulnerable and overexposed, and the gathering may seem more a collection of a few individuals than a group.

With too many, it may be difficult to maintain intimacy and a level of participation: some may become lost in the crowd. In practical terms, it may not be easy to sit together and maintain easy eye-contact with everyone else. People may need to pray out more loudly so all can hear, which can be hard for some to remember and others to do. You could offset this by breaking up the group into twos or threes, but being limited to that particular approach could fragment the group.

The leadership style of a larger group becomes more 'front-led' by necessity. In a smaller group, the leader can be more of an informal co-ordinator. And while a small group can be a good place to test out members' ministries, others may not be so eager to take a turn at leading prayer if the group's size makes the prospect too daunting.

Group setting

Numbers can be a factor here too. A small group meets comfortably in a home. A large group may find it more of a squeeze, often not a problem for teenagers or students, but perhaps an issue for adults and those of maturer years. What impact might physical proximity and limited personal space have on praying together?

Prayer in a relaxed home setting can feel more open and intimate, and encourage greater active participation than is possible in a Sunday service. There is also a more obvious link between prayer and the everyday, as the activity is moved outside designated worship space into living space.

Using a more overtly 'holy' setting within the church building could create a more sacred ambience, though you might find it engenders a holy hush that inhibits verbal participation.

Finally, what impact might the formality of a neutral meeting room have on group prayer? Will your room feel too impersonal, or will its freedom from homely distractions be an advantage? If using such a room, you may wish to consider the positioning of furniture and people for your prayer time, especially where the group is meeting for a teaching session of some kind. Will you all stay put to pray, or rearrange yourselves? Will you be praying on straight-backed chairs or cushioned sofas? What difference might that make?

Group background

The spiritual experience of group members needs to be borne in mind. Are they used to spontaneous, spoken prayer, or more familiar with set liturgy and silence? This does not mean you should not expand people's horizons. A group can be the very place to explore different modes of prayer, but being sensitive to where people are starting from will affect *how* you introduce new things.

Meaningful prayer in a small group will inevitably challenge members to greater participation and deeper personal disclosure, but people do not necessarily respond at the same rate. Encouraging openness while respecting people's privacy and pace may need careful managing, particularly at the beginning of a group's life, when you are looking to build and establish trust. The confidentiality of shared prayer needs may be a crucial issue for some, and it is helpful to address this directly early on.

Also, our differing personality types mean some ways of praying engage us, while others leave us cold. For some, the physical action of lighting a candle helps them 'see' their prayer; for others, the candle's symbolic aspect – perhaps as the light of hope in a dark world – will be most captivating. Some temperaments find background music a help; for others, it's a distraction. Some will want to participate in spoken word or action; others will relish the opportunity for stillness.

Your own personality type and background also play their part in the sort of prayer you feel comfortable facilitating.

Praying in small groups: choosing the threads

In selecting the threads for our prayer tapestry, we focus on what and how we want to communicate.

The things we say to one another in ordinary life – thank you, sorry, please – mirror areas of communication to God. Leading prayer means giving opportunities for these things to be said through praise and thanksgiving, confession, intercession and petition. It also means enabling things to be heard and received through silence or reflection and resting in God's presence. You'll not be able to choose every thread for each prayer time any more than you'd expect all elements of communication to be reflected in every human conversation.

The second set of prayer threads comprises the different ways of praying: with words, set or spontaneous; actions or postures; with music or silence; with visual aids or empty hands; speaking or listening; doing or being.

Given all this choice and the variety of personalities in any group, you may feel dismayed by the impossibility of pleasing everyone all of the time. But I hope instead you'll find your appetite whetted for introducing different ways of praying. You may open doors for those who've never felt they are any 'good' at prayer, often those who see themselves as practical hands-on types rather than spiritually gifted and reflective.

If you do explore new territory, encourage people to go with you, even in activities they don't quite see as 'their thing'. God can meet us powerfully where we least expect it and through means we'd never have chosen. We tend to feel less in control when we pray outside our preferred ways of operating, which leaves God more room for manoeuvre and space to come in.

So acknowledge that perhaps not everyone will find every prayer time comfortable, but ask people to remain patient and open. Difficulties in prayer can create potential for growth as we push back our boundaries and flex our spiritual muscles.

The craft of leading prayer

Be prepared

The best way to prepare for leading prayer is to be someone who prays regularly yourself, building the relationship with God that you're wanting to foster in the particular activity you're leading.

But more practical preparation is important too. Try the activity for yourself beforehand so you have a feel for how it works and have spotted any potential glitches. Make sure you have enough of whatever you need to go round. If you're using a CD player or equivalent, make sure it's working and test out the appropriate volume setting.

Encourage participation

We're often tempted to judge people's level of participation in prayer by how much they speak up, but there are other ways of enabling people to take part in prayer. Some are daunted by praying out loud, but can be encouraged to 'break the sound barrier' by using a set form of words to say individually or together – lack of spontaneity need not mean lack of sincerity!

Actions may also speak louder than words in prayer as in human relationships. An activity such as lighting a candle can be profoundly meaningful where sensitively introduced. It can enable group members to express something outwardly that is personal, without exposing what they need to remain private. This may be particularly valuable in a newly formed group where people do not know one another, and are still at the stage of building trust. It is also useful where the group represents a wide range of spirituality and experience.

Finally, moving beyond words can help 'even up' a group that has become dominated by the eloquent extroverts, who may – often unintentionally – subdue others by their enthusiasm for praying out loud.

Give it space

While we wouldn't think of starting a romantic tête-à-tête with a loved one by dashing through the door with our mind on other things, a group's prayer time can too often get squeezed into the end of a busy meeting and then done in a rush. But prayer, like any communication at depth, needs time.

Decide what proportion of the meeting is needed for the prayer activity, and keep the group to those boundaries. Save that personal pastoral issue or that fascinating red herring for the coffee time!

Be sensitive to pace

You can set the tone of the prayers by using a calm, warm and measured speaking voice. Ensure your instructions for any activity are as brief and simple as possible. An over-complicated introduction distracts from the prayer itself and people become restless. (If your activity needs so much explaining, it may be too elaborate in the first place!) Help people engage with the prayer time by guiding them to settle quietly – using a verse of Scripture, or inviting them to adopt a comfortable, but alert, posture. It can be helpful for people to focus their attention on their breathing: they can take a few moments to deliberately 'breathe out' their concerns and distractions, and gently 'breathe in' the presence of God.

'Pacing' silence may feel awkward to begin with, but stay calm: this will help people relax. If you are uncomfortable with silence, they will pick up your tension. The best way to gauge an appropriate length for a period of silence, when you have invited people to make a response within it, is to make the same response yourself. Actively participating gives you a feel for the time that's needed. Remember that what seems like a long silence to the leader can actually seem much shorter and full of inner activity for those praying.

Invite feedback

Sometimes it will be appropriate for the group to share their experiences of a prayer activity afterwards. These are often the times when you realize how busy a silence can be, or how much can come out of a simple action or form of words. It's also a way of discovering how effective a particular prayer exercise has been for the group, as well as highlighting members' different prayer preferences and personalities.

Invite, but don't insist on, feedback. Sometimes groups or individuals are not ready to open up in this way; others may have had a profound experience that they're not quite able to put into words at all.

Music or silence?

Appropriate music can be a wonderful backdrop to praying together. It can help soothe the spirit, create a peaceful atmosphere and muffle any potentially distracting tummy-rumblings and clock-tickings. Where used, music should be played quietly, and you should not have to raise your voice unnecessarily over it.

However, some people find even music something of an intrusion, and prefer total silence. It's worth experimenting with both approaches, and finding out from your group how music or silence affects their prayer response.

13

It's not all down to you!

Group prayer is, as its title says, a corporate activity, and a joint responsibility. As you lead prayers, do your part in guiding and encouraging, but allow and enable the participation of others.

When you open up a prayer activity, you are creating space for people to make their own response to God. It can feel hard to step back and let this happen, but do not succumb to the temptation to jump in and take over. Have faith and trust that God is eager to commune with his people. Play your part in leading prayers, but don't forget to leave something for God to do!

Using the ideas

The following prayer ideas encompass a range of approaches from practical hands-on to led meditations, and from invitations to spontaneous words to suggestions for set words. The aim is to reflect the diversity of prayer possible in a small group, with the hope that they will contain the ebullient, enable the hesitant, and open up some new avenues of communicating with God.

The ideas may need to be adapted to take account of your particular group and its needs. You may also wish to tailor the suggestions to fit in with other aspects of your group's meeting, or even use just one part of a suggestion to simplify your prayer activity. Please pick up these ideas as you wish and use them as a springboard for your own. Each group is unique and will develop its own prayer preferences and patterns.

This material could also be a resource if you're sharing the leading of prayer around group members. For some this might be the first step into leading intercessions in a church service.

Others may discover a particular flair for leading group prayer in itself.

Part 1 contains ideas for different prayer elements that may be incorporated into the group meeting.

Part 2 is thematically based on seasons of the church year. These ideas could also be used 'out of season' if the theme fits your group's agenda.

A section on **Further resources** provides some suggestions you might find helpful in developing group prayer.

The **Index of Bible references** and the **Index of themes** give prayer suggestion numbers (shown in brackets throughout the book) rather than page numbers.

Part 1

THREADING PRAYER
THROUGH THE MEETING

1

Beginnings and endings

(1) WHAT HAVE WE BROUGHT?

People often arrive at meetings physically, but with their minds on something else. This exercise can help 'clear the ground', so everyone is free to give their full attention to the group.

You will need a cross to stand on the floor or table, and a basket of assorted stones.
 Some gentle music could be a helpful background to the reflective time.

As people arrive, ask them to take a stone from the basket. Once everyone is gathered, tell people their stone is to represent whatever they have brought to the meeting, and will form part of the opening prayer time. Explain that you are going to allow the group some moments for holding, feeling and reflecting on what their stone means to them personally. Then invite them to come forward and lay their stone at the foot of the cross. If people wish, they can accompany the action with an appropriate short prayer such as '**Lord, I trust _____ to your care**' or '**This stone represents _____ that I lay at the foot of your Cross**', and so on.

Note

Stones could stand for burdens and concerns, stepping stones and stumbling blocks; precious treasures or long-standing difficulties. Dependent on the group, you may wish to prompt their imagination by mentioning such possibilities.

You may also want to come back to the stones at the end of the meeting. Do people want to take them away, or leave them there? And if they do pick the stones up now, do they feel different?

(2) HIS PRESENCE IN THE PRESENT

When our attention is caught up in past or future concerns, it blocks our availability to Christ who meets us in the here and now. This exercise is one way of coming back to focus on the present moment, and could also be used by group members during the week.

The prayer leader guides the prayers

As you sit, close your eyes and settle yourself into a posture that is comfortable but alert ... Rest your hands on your lap, and enjoy the stillness after all the movement of the day ... Christ Jesus is Lord over all that has been, all that is, and all that is to come, but we meet him in the present moment. So we want to bring our whole selves to him now ... Clench both your hands into fists ... Become aware of all the things from past moments and days that occupy your thoughts and feelings right now ... Imagine you are holding them all tight in your left hand ... A closed hand leaves no space for Christ to come in ... So in your own time, relax your hand into an open, upturned palm, releasing these past matters into Christ's care ... Now become aware of all the concerns you have about what is to come – worries, things to

20

do, even things you're looking forward to . . . Imagine you are holding them clenched in your right hand . . . A clenched hand means a tension that can be tiring . . . So in your own time, open out your hand as an act of letting these concerns go into Christ's keeping, and trusting him with the outcome . . . Open hands express a willingness to respond and receive whatever Christ wants to fill you with here and now . . . Stay for a moment in quiet, with palms upturned, consciously in his presence in the present moment, offering this time, this place, this meeting, yourself, to him, for him to use as he chooses . . . Christ Jesus is Lord over all that has been, all that is, and all that is to come . . . And he is with us now . . . Thanks be to God.

(3) COLOURS ON THE CROSS

You will need two pieces of paper, preferably of flipchart size, on each of which you have drawn the outline of a large cross. You will also need felt-tip pens of assorted colours and thicknesses.

Some suitable background music, such as Pachelbel's Canon, will enhance this exercise.

Put the first piece of paper, plus pens, on a central table.

Explain that we can come to Jesus just as we are, with our particular personalities, moods and experiences. Ask the group to take a moment to reflect on how they are approaching Jesus at this moment. What do they bring? How do they feel? How might they use colours, lines or shapes to express these things? For example, have they come in a peaceful 'blue' frame of mind, or a more passionate 'red'? Do they feel spiky, or dotty, or in a swirl? Do they see themselves as a solid block of colour or hollow and airy?

As the background music plays, invite people to express how and who they are today before God by using the felt-tip pens to make coloured marks, shapes or doodles within the outline of the cross. Allow the music to continue until everyone has had an opportunity to add their own colours on to the cross.

Draw this time to a close by thanking God that, in Jesus, he receives every aspect of who we are and transforms us into whom he wants us to become. The colourful patterns created on the cross could also be seen as the group 'stained-glass window'. Ask for the light of Christ to shine through all the colours and shapes we have just brought to him together.

At the end of the meeting, repeat the exercise using the second cross. Have people's feelings and perceptions changed throughout the session? Do they want to repeat their colour and pattern, or do they find themselves drawing something different now? Thank Jesus that he is always at work, making all things new, at his pace and for his purposes, and finish by joining in the Grace together.

(4) SINS SHREDDED

Confession together can be a useful, though difficult, thing to do. This approach enables the group to acknowledge their need of forgiveness before one another without being forced to expose personal details.

You will need an electric paper shredder, paper and pens. You also need to give each person a copy of the following set of verses:

Jesus says, 'Friend, your sins are forgiven.' (Luke 5.20)
Your sins have been forgiven on account of his name. (1 John 2.12)

There is now no condemnation for those who are in Christ Jesus.
  (Romans 8.1)
Jesus says, 'If the Son sets you free you will be free indeed.' (John
  8.36)

Read 1 John 1.9: 'If we confess our sins he who is faithful
and just will forgive us our sins and cleanse us from all
unrighteousness.' Ask each person to write down privately and
penitently any action or area where they want to ask for God's
forgiveness. Then invite them to come and push their paper
through the shredder as a reminder of how completely God
has dealt with our sins in Christ.

Next, ask people to form pairs. Each person reads their copy
of the distributed Bible verses prayerfully, and selects the one
they sense is most appropriate for their partner. Pairs then
take it in turns to read the chosen verse to one another, with as
much personal warmth and eye contact as they can offer.

(5) ACTS OF PRAYER

This exercise uses a familiar prayer acronym in a slightly
different way. The group's agility, embarrassment factor and
available space will determine how you lead this activity. It can
be done entirely seated.

Explain that as we bring our whole selves into prayer, we can
speak to God through body language as well as words. So we
will follow the ACTS prayer format (Adoration, Confession,
Thanksgiving, Supplication), using gestures and posture instead of speech. We can offer whatever gestures are meaningful to us as our personal prayer, with no anxieties about what
is 'right' or 'wrong'.

The prayer leader guides the prayers

As you sit, close your eyes and settle quietly, so you are relaxed, but alert. Bring your hands on to your lap and move
them so that the palms are upwards, with fingers gently
touching, like an open flower ready to receive the sunshine
. . . Now slowly turn your face upwards to heaven . . . Let go
of other concerns and simply be attentive to the present
moment . . . Stay like this for a few moments as an expression
of your openness to God.

We continue our prayer with Adoration . . . So in your own
time, move yourself gently into a gesture that expresses sheer
adoration of the Lord . . . Stay in this position for a few moments, allowing your whole being to be caught up in adoring
him . . . Now we move into the Confession part of our
prayer . . . So as you are ready, gently adopt a gesture that
expresses an attitude of confession for those things you know
need to be put right before the Lord . . . Remain focused in
this position for some moments . . . The Lord forgives the
penitent . . . So now gradually move back into the receiving
gesture with which we started our prayers – resting hands with
open palms, and face turned up to heaven . . . receiving his
forgiveness and renewal . . . In response, we move into
Thanksgiving . . . Slowly adopt a bodily gesture through which
you express an attitude of thanksgiving to the Lord . . . And
stay with it for a few moments . . . We have much to be thankful for . . . Finally, we make our requests in prayer, as we offer
Supplications to the Lord . . . Move yourself gently into a
posture that expresses a supplicating, asking stance before
the Lord . . . Hold it for a few moments, sustaining your
prayer . . . Finally, when you are ready, open your eyes . . . as
we join hands as a group to express our unity in Christ . . .
Enjoying our fellowship and presence together in prayer for a
few moments . . . Amen.

(6) SEALED WITH LOVE

You will need some oil for anointing. A massage oil, or ordinary baby oil, could be used.

The prayer leader reads Isaiah 43.1–3.

After this, the group passes round the anointing oil. Each person takes the oil and anoints his or her neighbour on the forehead (or on the wrists, if that seems more appropriate for the group). While doing this, the one anointing prays a prayer to seal the neighbour personally in God's love; e.g.: '**Helen, the Lord says "I have called you by name. You are mine."**'

(7) COMMENDING TO CHRIST

If time is short in a meeting, here is a brief way of praying for one another before coffee. This can be especially helpful if you're seated in a circle or at round tables.

As this exercise includes asking people to focus on something they appreciate about a fellow group member, you might encourage them to pass it on to the person concerned afterwards.

The prayer leader guides the prayers

Close your eyes and take some calm, deep breaths to help you become settled . . . Where two or three are gathered in his name, Jesus promises to be in the midst . . . Seek to become quietly sensitive to his presence here and now . . . Take some moments to remain aware of the presence of Jesus, and the presence of the group around you . . . Now direct your attention by bringing into your mind's eye the person sitting to the right of you, created and loved by God . . . Think of something about that person that you really appreciate, and silently thank the Lord for that quality or gift . . . Now shift your focus, and bring into your mind's eye the person on your left . . . God has called them into being and known them by name from the beginning . . . In your imagination, bring that person to Jesus and see them held in his loving presence . . . As you continue to see them there, pray that he will bless them abundantly, and meet them right now at the point of their deepest need . . . As you come to the end of this prayer, become aware of the wider group, and when you are ready, open your eyes to see them around you . . . We can express our unity in Christ Jesus and continue to bless one another by joining hands and saying the Grace together to one another in our words, looks and smiles . . .

All: **May the grace of our Lord Jesus Christ, and the love of God and the fellowship of the Holy Spirit be with us all evermore. Amen.**

(8) TOTALLY ENFOLDED

You will need a small bowl filled with sand, and a bowl of water, plus a small towel.

The group passes round the bowl of sand. Each time it is passed on, the person receiving the bowl holds it out as the person who passed it licks a finger and dips it into the sand, leaving sand-grains stuck to the fingertip.

Once the bowl has been passed round, ask everyone to look at their fingertips and try to count the grains of sand they can see there. Meanwhile, read the psalmist's trusting prayer in Psalm 139.17–18:

'How weighty to me are your thoughts, O God! How vast is
   the sum of them!
I try to count them – they are more than the sand;
I come to the end – I am still with you.'

Allow the group some moments to reflect on the amazing truth
that we are each held in the Lord's thoughts in ways that infin-
itely outnumber the many sand-grains on our fingertips alone.

   Explain that not only are we totally surrounded by the Lord's
loving thoughts, we are also completely cleansed by his forgiveness. Read the psalmist's confident prayer in Psalm 51.1–2, 7:

'Have mercy on me, O God, according to your steadfast love;
according to your abundant mercy, blot out my transgressions.
Wash me thoroughly from my iniquity, and cleanse me
   from my sin.
Purge me with hyssop, and I shall be clean; wash me, and
   I shall be whiter than snow.'

To help everyone reflect on this amazing truth, the first person
in the group washes his or her hands in the bowl of water, and
then holds it out for the next person to do the same, and so on
round the group.

   Conclude with a led prayer, thanking the Lord for totally
enfolding his children in his care and forgiveness.

(9) PASS THE SALT

You will need a full salt shaker.

Read Mark 9.50: 'Salt is good; but if salt has lost its saltiness,
how can you season it? Have salt in yourselves, and be at
peace with one another',

and Colossians 4.6:

'Let your speech always be gracious, seasoned with salt, so that you may know how you ought to answer everyone.'

As we go out into the world, we're called to be a Christian presence that brings out the fullness and flavour of life to those around us for the sake of Christ.

Ask the group to settle into quietness and to bring to mind one place they frequent in their everyday lives where they want to be more spiritually salty in what they say and how they act. Invite people simply to name these places out loud as prayers of gathering these places under God's rule.

Now move on to prayers of sending out the group into these places for Christ. Each one shakes out a little salt into the open hands of the next person, who receives it and eats it as the salt-giver prays for that person:

May your words and deeds be a savour for the Saviour wherever he calls you.

Continue until the salt has been passed right round the group. As Christ commands us both to have salt in ourselves, *and* to be at peace with one another, the group may wish to end the prayer time by sharing the Peace.

(10) PRAYER CAN

This exercise can be an effective, simple way of incorporating prayer into the end of a meeting, as people leave their prayers behind. It could also generate some encouragement, and perhaps discussion on answered and unanswered prayer in future weeks.

You will need an empty ring-pull drinks can, some small pieces of paper and pens.

Explain that where we feel frustrated because we can't do anything more to resolve a particular problem or concern, prayer can. We remind ourselves of this by using a Prayer Can for this prayer activity.

Distribute paper and pens and ask people to write a short prayer expressing some need or issue where they feel at the end of their own resources, and then to fold their piece of paper up small. Pass the Prayer Can round the group, and ask everyone to post their prayers into it.

Show the group that once these pieces of paper are in the can, it's very difficult to get them out again. In the same way, we are to leave our prayers in Jesus' care, and not struggle or strive to take matters back into our own hands.

Challenge the group to let go of their particular prayer concern this week, and resist the temptation to work or worry at it. They are simply to remind themselves that they have committed it to the Prayer Can.

Keep the Prayer Can to bring out at a following meeting. Ask for feedback on what has happened regarding the prayers people placed in it.

Note

You might prefer to use this exercise specifically for confession prayers, as a way of helping people let go and trust that their sins have been fully forgiven and dealt with through Christ. In this case you could complete the prayer time by crushing the can and placing it in a rubbish bin.

29

(11) SIT, WALK, STAND

You will need sheets of A4 paper, plus writing materials such as felt-tip pens.

You will also need a selection of promises from the Bible written out on a sheet. These might include:

My steadfast love shall not depart from you. (Isaiah 54.10)
I will never leave you or forsake you. (Hebrews 13.5)
You did not choose me but I chose you. (John 15.16)
I am with you always. (Matthew 28.20)
My power is made perfect in weakness. (2 Corinthians 12.9)

Give everyone a sheet of paper and invite people to write on it a Bible promise from the selection (or another verse of personal significance to them, if preferred). They should write it across the whole sheet.

Next, ask them to find a spot on the floor, a little way from where they are sitting, and place the paper on the ground, face-up.

Once all have done this and returned to their seats, move into prayer.

The prayer leader guides the meditation

Close your eyes . . . As you sit, bring your attention on your feet, resting on the ground . . . First focus on the left foot . . . and your toes . . . Starting with the little toe, become aware of the sensation of each toe in turn . . . Now move your attention along the outside of your foot . . . and then to the heel . . . Let your left foot relax on the floor . . . Now focus on your right foot . . . and your toes . . . Starting with the little toe, become aware of the sensation of each toe in turn . . . Now move your attention along the outside of your foot . . . and then to the heel . . . Let your right foot relax on the floor . . . As you sit in God's presence and rest your feet, think about the times you will rest this week . . . Will you make space for stillness, or try to keep moving? . . . Just for the moment, be still and know that he is God . . . And commit your resting to the Lord in the week ahead . . .

After your feet have carried you away from here, you will walk to many places in the week ahead . . . Think about some of these places . . . The Bible tells us that 'Whoever says, "I abide in Christ," ought to walk just as he walked.'* . . . How do you walk? . . . In a rush or dragging your feet? . . . Slouching or tense? . . . As those loved by the Lord we can walk tall, at peace and at his pace . . . Practise this walk of faith now . . . In your own time, open your eyes, get up from your seat, walk over to your 'promise' paper sheet, and stand on it . . . Focus on how you are walking . . . and commit your walking to the Lord in the week ahead . . .

Close your eyes again as you stand on the promise you wrote out . . . Reflect for a few moments on why you chose it and what it means to you . . . Think about where you might be called to take a stand on its truth in the week ahead . . . those personal situations known to you and the Lord where you need to stand firm as his child . . . Offer them to him as they come to mind . . . and imagine yourself in those situations, confident and grounded on the truth of God's promises . . . What difference will that make? . . . Commit your standing to the Lord in the week ahead . . .

When you're ready, pick up your promise and hold it, as we close with a prayer of blessing:

* 1 John 2.6

31

May we rest in the protection of the Father,
may we walk in the presence of the Son,
may we stand in the power of the Spirit.
Amen.

Note

Depending on your group and meeting room, you may wish to omit the walking section of the meditation for practical reasons. If so, you could begin the exercise by asking people to place their 'promise' under their feet as they sit. But do include the invitation for people to imagine and commit their walking to the Lord in prayer, even if the only actual physical movement they do is to stand up.

(12) GO, GROW AND GLOW

This exercise can be useful at the end of an evening meeting or discipleship course. People are free to make a personal response to 'seal' what they take away from the session(s), by using all or any of the actions offered as appropriate.

You will need a small pot of earth, some seeds (pumpkin seeds are a good size), tea-light candles, a bunch of dry twigs, and a small standing cross. You will also need some reflective music to play as a background to this exercise.

Place everything centrally round the cross. Explain that as the course/evening has ended, group members are invited to make their own personal prayer in response to whatever they sense God is particularly asking of them. They can express this prayer by one of three actions:

If there is something in their life that needs to *Go*, they can break a twig and place it by the cross.

If there is something in their life God wants to *Grow* in them, they can take a seed and plant it in the pot of earth.

If there is something in their life God wants to *Glow* (i.e. a gift or quality that needs to be more fully expressed), they can light a candle near the cross.

Play the music and allow people the opportunity, when they feel ready, to make their responses.

Close with some words committing these prayers to the Lord. You may wish to end this time by saying the Grace together.

2

Praise and thanksgiving

---◆◆◆---

(13) PSALM PRAISE AND RESPONSE

You will need to ensure each person has a Bible or a copy of Psalm 97. Some suitably joyous music to play in the background can also help 'lift' the praise very effectively.

Once the music is playing, each person reads a verse of the psalm in turn, going round the group. After each verse, everyone declares together:

All: **Almighty God, we gaze on your greatness.**

Allow the music to run on for a little while after the end of the spoken praise, to enable people to continue gazing at the greatness of God in silent adoration.

Note

A variation on reading round the group is simply to invite whoever feels led to pick up with the next verse of the psalm. In theory this sounds awkward, but this open form of reading can work powerfully. People's anxieties about cutting in on one another with the same verse can be allayed by reassuring the group that it's perfectly acceptable for several voices to read together (though it does help if it's from the same version!). In practice, however, such confusion rarely happens, or if it does, it's remarkable how the particular verse is often highly appropriate for several voices to declare in unison.

(14) DIY PSALM

You will need enough pens and paper for everyone, some suitable background music to play during the prayer itself, and any concluding words you wish the group to say together.

Distribute pens and paper and explain that the group is going to create a psalm of praise and thanksgiving together, with everyone contributing a verse. Ask each person to write down a one-sentence prayer either of praise – worshipping God for some aspect of who he is (loving, faithful, powerful, etc.), or of thanksgiving – offering gratitude for something he has done, in which the whole group can share. Reassure people that, as in the Psalms, simple, direct prayers can be the most effective.

Once the verses have been written, put on the music and invite each person to read their verse in turn. You might like to finish with the group joining together in saying words such as:

Glory to the Father, and to the Son and to the Holy Spirit.
As it was in the beginning, is now and ever shall be.
World without end, Amen.

(15) BOUQUET OF PRAISE

You will need a bunch of cut flowers, and a vase. Place these in the middle of the group.

Introduce the prayers by explaining that the flowers will form a picture of how our praises and thanksgivings are a fragrant and beautiful offering to God.

Ask people to think of something they wish to thank or praise God for. Then invite people to speak out their prayer, placing a flower in the vase as they do so. When the prayers have finished and all the flowers are used up, a visual bouquet of worship remains in the middle as a continuing source of pleasure.

You could use Psalm 145 as an alternative to extempore prayer: each person in turn reads a verse and places a flower in the vase.

(16) ALPHABET PRAISE

Introduce this exercise by referring to Jesus' words in Revelation 22.12: '**I am the Alpha and the Omega, the first and the last, the beginning and the end.**'

Explain that as Jesus declares he is Lord of all by using the first and last letters of the Greek alphabet, so we will offer him our praises through the letters of our alphabet.

Invite the group to pray in turn by saying a short prayer of praise for some aspect of Jesus. The first person starts with the letter A, and the group continues to pray through the alphabet letter by letter, going round the room. After each individual prayer, everyone joins in a response together:

Person praying:	Lord, we praise you that you are Almighty, Blessed, Compassionate, etc. . . .
All:	Lord, from beginning to end, we praise your name.

Since some letters will yield more aspects for praise than others, you may wish to continue with one letter round the

36

room until you have exhausted its possibilities, before moving on to the next one.

Note

This simple exercise could also be used to move from praise of God himself to thanksgivings for what God has given and done. Special creativity and ingenuity may be called for with certain letters of the alphabet – with xylophones and zebras perhaps exciting particular gratitude!

(17) RAINBOW PRAISE

The sequence of colours in the rainbow – red, orange, yellow, green, blue, indigo and violet – is often remembered through the traditional mnemonic 'Richard of York Gave Battle In Vain'. The shared response in the following prayers forms a Christian mnemonic for recalling God's rainbow colours.

You will need lengths of ribbon in colours corresponding to the rainbow, and a large white candle.

Roll the ribbons up and arrange them in rainbow order round the candle's base.

You will also need to have copies of, or introduce, the response.

Explain that we are going to praise God through all the colours of the rainbow. The colours combined make up the white, pure, shining light of God in Christ, represented by the candle.

The rainbow itself represents God's mercy to his people, in the covenant of love extended to Noah and fulfilled through the saving grace of Christ.

Light the candle and open the prayer by reading God's rainbow promise in Genesis 9:12–17.

Unroll the red ribbon, and invite prayers of thanksgiving and praise linked to whatever that colour inspires, from red itself to anything associated with it. Encourage a creative and imaginative openness to whatever the Spirit might bring to mind. Bring these prayers to a close by leading the shared response:

Leader: Lord, we praise and thank you for the
All: **Riches Of Your Grace, Beautiful In Victory.**

Now unroll the orange ribbon, and repeat the process, ending with the shared response. When all the colours have been unfurled, spend some time thanking God for what the whole rainbow means to us: God's faithfulness to his promises through sunshine and rain, the beauty of his creation, etc.

Close by drawing together the different colours of your shared prayer in saying the Grace together.

(18) REMINDERS OF YOU

Prepare for this exercise a week ahead by asking group members to bring to the next meeting some item that reminds them of some aspect of God.

Some gentle background music could be helpful to this exercise.

Place a tray in the middle of the group, and ask everyone to have their items to hand.

Open the prayer by asking people one by one to place their item on the tray and offer a simple prayer that expresses what it says to them about God: e.g. 'Thank you, Lord, for this comb that reminds me how all the hairs on our head are numbered by you', etc. Once the item is placed on the tray, allow some moments for all to reflect on the object and the accompanying prayer. Conclude each section with:

Leader: Lord, we praise you for all you are.
All: **We thank you for all you have created.**

Continue like this until all the objects are on the tray, and the response has been spoken for the final time. Afterwards you may want to encourage people to discuss their responses to the different objects, and offer any further insights that emerged during the prayer time.

Note

An alternative to having the group provide items is to put together your own tray of objects – perhaps incorporating items that appeal to the senses of taste, touch and smell as well as sight. In this case, you could open the prayer with some time for reflection, and then invite short, simple prayers where people give thanks for the particular insights and aspects of God that have been prompted by the objects in front of them.

(19) 'WHAT DO THESE STONES MEAN?'

Stones are a valuable prayer resource, as they are used to mean so many things in the Bible: They can represent God's people (Joshua 4.5, Matthew 16.18, 1 Peter 2.5, Revelation 2.17), and Jesus himself (1 Corinthians 10.4, 1 Peter 2.6–8). They can form boundaries (Deuteronomy 19.14), blocks (Lamentations 3.9, Matthew 27.60), buildings (1 Kings 7.9–12, Revelation 21.18–21), or burdens (Proverbs 27.3). They can be treasures (Isaiah 54.11–12), tablets (Exodus 24.12), or in need of transformation (Ezekiel 36.26). They can be used to protect (Psalm 18.2) or attack (1 Samuel 17.50, John 8.59).

Stones bring solidity to our prayers. We can hold them, and the stones themselves can 'hold' our concerns, people, and prayers beyond words.

All the above may well inspire your own creativity with stones in your group's prayer life. In the suggestion below, stones become a memorial of God's activity in our lives. This can be particularly helpful at the start of a new year or term, as people recall what God has done over the previous season as an encouragement to go on in faith.

You will need a selection of stones in a basket, plus a tray placed centrally.

Explain that Scripture often reminds us to look back at how God has acted in our lives to strengthen our faith for the journey ahead. For example, as the Israelites finally entered the Promised Land, God parted the waters so they could cross the river Jordan. Joshua commanded that twelve stones be taken from the river bed (one stone for each tribe), and carried to where the Israelites set up camp at Gilgal.

Read Joshua 4.19–24, and explain that in our prayers we will make our own 'Gilgal' pile of memorial stones.

Open the prayers by asking people to reflect on the way God has brought them over the past week or year, and bring to mind something he has done in their lives that they want to give thanks for and remember. As these things occur – large or small – they choose a stone from the basket and place it on the tray. They can do this as a silent prayer to 'mark the spot' of God's blessing, or offer a short prayer out loud: **'Lord, thank you for . . .'**

Continue until either the prayers or the stones have run out, and offer a concluding prayer, such as:

**Thank you Lord, that you are the one who was, is now, and
shall be for ever.**
May we treasure all you have done in our past,
May we turn to all you are in our present,
May we trust you for all you will do in our future.
Amen.

(20) LIVING STONES

*You will need a selection of stones, and a cross or large white
candle.*

*You will also need a CD track of lively praise music, classical
or contemporary, according to what suits your group.*

Place the cross or lighted candle on a central table, and explain
that this represents Christ. Pass the stones round the group
and ask people to choose the one they wish to use to represent
them.

Remind people that we draw close to God as we worship
him through our praises and thanksgivings. Psalm 100.4 calls
us to **'Enter his gates with thanksgiving, and his courts with
praise. Give thanks to him, bless his name.'**

Ask everyone to place their stones on the table in front of
them. Explain that worshipful music will be played for the
duration of the prayer time. Ask people to listen to it, and as
they do so, to allow to come to mind aspects of God that they
want to praise, or things he has done in their lives that they
want to thank him for. As things occur, they respond by
offering a silent prayer of praise or thanksgiving, and moving
their stone closer to the cross – a little way or a long way as
appropriate.

Once you have started the music, allow these prayers to
continue for some minutes, or until the piece of music comes
to a natural end.

Finish by looking at the stones and reflecting on how they are now all closer to Christ at the centre, even if some have moved further than others on this particular occasion; each personal journey towards Christ has its own unique pace and timing. This is a picture of what happens as we worship. In fact, the picture is incomplete: God promises that as we draw near to him, he draws near to us, so our worship is a two-way movement towards a deeper encounter with him.

It's also worth observing how the stones are now also closer to one another as well as Christ. As God's people, his living stones, join in worship, we are built together in loving fellowship to form a temple for the presence of God among us.

(21) WHAT'S IN A NAME?

You will need to write out on pieces of coloured card the names of Jesus; e.g.: Prince of Peace, Good Shepherd, Bread of Life, Living Word, Light of the World, etc. Some gentle music is also valuable for this exercise.

Place the cards blank side up in the middle of the group, and invite each person to take one.

As background music is played, ask people to reflect quietly on the name they have drawn. What does it reveal about who Jesus is? What does it mean? Where might they need to hear that particular name spoken into a personal situation or one known to them? Encourage the group not to work too hard at analysing the name, but to allow the Holy Spirit to bring things to mind and make the appropriate connections.

Draw this time to a close, and invite people, if they wish, to share the name they were given and what emerged for them as they reflected on it.

Conclude with a brief time of prayer together. Ask people to contribute by putting their card in the middle, face up this time, alongside some straightforward words of thanksgiving, such as, **'Lord, thank you that you are the Beginning and the End'**, etc.

(22) SONGS OF PRAISE

We can too easily sing the words of hymns or songs in church without due care and attention. By slowing the pace and taking time to ponder the content of some familiar sung words, we may discover richer layers of meaning within. We may even find ourselves becoming more thoughtful about what we sing on a Sunday.

You will need to select a hymn or song of praise suitable for your group, and have a copy of it for each person. Your choice should comprise several verses that offer some food for thought and reflection in between. Some possibilities might be: 'Praise, my soul, the King of heaven'; 'Immortal, invisible, God only wise'; 'When I survey the wondrous cross'; 'Meekness and majesty'; 'In Christ alone'.

You will also need some gentle background instrumental music to accompany the exercise.

Explain that we'll be using the words of a well-known hymn or song of praise to prompt our own worship, in silence and out loud. While the words may be familiar, this prayer activity will give us the space to absorb them at a deeper level, and allow them to become a springboard for our own responses of praise and thanksgiving.

Distribute the copies of your chosen hymn or song. Start the music and read the first verse. Leave some moments for people to read it over and reflect quietly, and then invite them to add their own prayers of praise in response, either silently or out loud. Some may simply wish to express their praises by repeating a line from the verse itself to make it their own prayer.

Continue until you have completed the hymn, allowing time for reflection and response after each verse. You may prefer to invite different group members to read the verses, as long as you ensure that appropriate space is left in between.

An effective way to end this prayer time is by singing the whole hymn through together rather than simply saying the Grace.

Encourage some feedback after this exercise. What did people gain from using familiar words in this way? Did it feel different to sing the hymn through having reflected on it? Could this affect how they approach singing in Sunday worship?

(23) COUNT YOUR BLESSINGS

You will need enough pipe cleaners for everyone, and plenty of assorted beads to thread on them. Both these items, in a variety of colours, should be obtainable at your local craft shop.

You will also need some gentle but uplifting background music to accompany this activity.

Explain that as we're often exhorted to 'count our blessings', we will do this literally in our prayer time.

Give each group member a pipe cleaner and invite people to call to mind a blessing that they want to thank the Lord for. As they think of one, they take a bead and thread it on to the pipe cleaner. People may want to choose beads of particular colours to stand for specific blessings.

Praise and thanksgiving

Encourage people to continue with this quietly as the music plays, to allow some space for personal blessings to come to mind that they may not previously have registered or perhaps have forgotten.

When the exercise seems to have reached its natural conclusion (or the beads are running out!), invite the group to offer short prayers of thanksgiving or praise based on the blessings their beads represent.

People may wish to take their counted blessings away with them afterwards, to help them remember how much they have to be thankful for.

3

Praying for our world

------◆◆◆------

(24) FEEDING THE NATIONS

Ask each group member to bring along a foodstuff that comes from, or is associated with, another part of the world.

Place the foods centrally, ensuring everyone knows what each one is and where it has come from.

Ask the group to pray short prayers out loud for the countries represented by the various foods. These can be simply naming the country and asking God's blessing upon it, but encourage people to use their imagination and let the foodstuffs themselves be a springboard for some prayerful creativity (e.g. a bunch of bananas might suggest prayers for fruitfulness; a packet of dry pasta might inspire intercession that hard hearts be softened by the water of life, etc.).

Once these prayers have finished, invite people to give thanks for the plentiful and varied supply of food we enjoy, and to pray for justice, that rich nations become more willing to share their resources with those who have less, so that all may have enough.

Afterwards, express a spirit of sharing by asking group members to take away a different foodstuff from the one they brought with them – and share it with someone else.

(25) PLASTICINE PRAYERS

While this idea may seem especially suitable for children, I first used it with a group of adults who greatly appreciated the opportunity for engaging in intercession with some hands-on activity. As one said afterwards, 'Thank you for giving us the opportunity to play.' Perhaps we too often underestimate the powerful combination of playfulness with prayerfulness.

You will need enough pieces of plasticine for each person to make the shapes that focus the prayers. Some very artistic plasticine bowls can emerge at the end of this exercise! People may wish to take these home with them as a reminder to stay open to God during the week.

The prayer leader guides the prayers

Work the plasticine in your hands and shape it into a ball

As this ball rests in your hand, imagine God holding our whole planet in the palms of *his* hands . . . Think about yourself living in this world, a tiny speck . . . Think about places that seem so far away, but from God's perspective are so near . . . So we pray for countries and areas of the world troubled by conflict or hardship – places distant from us but close to God's heart. Let's offer these places to the Lord by name . . .

Look at this ball again, and see it as a large stone, like the one rolled away from Jesus' tomb on Easter Day . . . Jesus is alive: the tombstone was moved, and Jesus' followers encountered their risen Lord . . . Let's pray for those we know who need to meet the living Lord Jesus, for whatever 'stone' that needs to be moved out of the way for them to see who he really is . . . Let's offer these people to the Lord by name . . .

Roll the ball between your palms so it becomes a long sausage/ spaghetti shape

By now you're probably finding your hands feel slightly grainy from contact with the plasticine . . . Let this be a reminder that God is not aloof from his world: he gets his hands dirty – and nail-scarred . . . So we pray for our nation and local community . . . The long shape can remind us that our society is stretched, stressed and strung out . . . Let's pray aloud or in silence for those we know who are under stress of whatever kind . . . (*Pause for open response . . . those in debt . . . overworked . . . etc.*).

The loose ends of our plasticine shape remind us that some in our society feel left out at the edges . . . Let's offer to the Lord people on the margins . . . (*Pause for open response . . . those living alone . . . unemployed . . . elderly . . . asylum seekers . . . etc.*).

Join the ends of the plasticine together to form a ring

Look at the circle you've formed, and think about the enfolding love of God that has no beginning and no end . . . There are those we know who need to experience the love of the Lord surrounding them and their circumstances especially right now . . . Let's name them before the Lord out loud or in silence . . .

Finally, use the plasticine to make a small bowl

It's much easier to mould the plasticine when it's warmed by our hands . . . This is how God works with us, warming us with his love so we become more flexible and open to him . . . Look at the bowl you have made . . . Scripture tells us that *we* are ordinary earthen vessels, or bowls, filled with the amazing life of Christ as his Spirit is poured into us . . . What sort of a bowl are you today – a bit leaky? . . . Or hard-baked? . . . Needing a few lumps and bumps smoothed out? . . . Hold the bowl in your hand, and be aware of the Lord's warming hands around you . . . Offer yourself to him to fill you with his Spirit and to shape you as he wills for his purposes . . . (*Pause*)

Formed by the Father, Forgiven by the Son, Filled with the Spirit,
We commit our all prayers to you, Lord. Amen.

(26) 'JULIAN' INTERCESSIONS, USING A HAZELNUT

You will need enough hazelnuts for each person to hold throughout the prayers, which open and close with words written by the four-teenth-century mystic, Julian of Norwich. Also hand out copies, or write on a large card, the words of response between each section.

The hazelnuts and response words are distributed.

The prayer leader guides the prayers

'The Lord showed me a little thing, the size of a hazelnut, on the palm of my hand. I looked at it thoughtfully and wondered, "What is this?" And the answer came, "It is all that is made." I marvelled that it continued to exist and did not suddenly disintegrate; it was so small. And again my mind supplied the answer, "It exists, both now and for ever, because God loves it." In short, everything owes its existence to the love of God.

In this "little thing" I saw three truths. The first is that God made it, the second is that God loves it, the third is that God sustains it . . . He is in truth Maker, Keeper and Lover.'

As you hold the nut, imagine God holding his whole created world in the palm of his hand, the world he has brought into being . . . So we pray for areas in our world that need to know the Maker's care (*invite the naming of places or world situations of conflict, or famine etc. . .*).

Leader: God is our Maker, Keeper and Lover.
All: **His goodness enfolds every one of his creatures and all his blessed works.**

As the hand keeps the nut from falling, imagine God protecting his vulnerable world through his mighty grasp. . . . Thank you, Lord, for the many ways you keep us from harm day by day. May we never take this gift for granted. And we pray for those who especially need to know the Keeper's power (*invite the naming of vulnerable groups, e.g. children, the elderly, the materially and spiritually poor, the exploited or abused . . . etc.*).

Leader: God is our Maker, Keeper and Lover.
All: **His goodness enfolds every one of his creatures and all his blessed works.**

As the warmth of your hand cherishes the nut, imagine God enfolding *all* people in his loving care, whoever and wherever they are. . . . We call to mind someone we know who needs the touch of the divine Lover's tenderness, and we pray for them to know the enfolding of God's love right now, even as we hold this nut in our hands. We name them out loud or silently and simply offer them into the Lord's hands . . .

Leader: God is our Maker, Keeper and Lover.
All: **His goodness enfolds every one of his creatures and all his blessed works.**

Finally, as the nut remains in your hand, imagine it represents a heart-felt longing that goes beyond words: a problem you can't solve; a person you feel unable to love or help, an area where you need to 'let go and let God'. . . . In quietness, open your hand and lift your concern to the Lord, asking him to be Maker, Keeper and Lover over this specific issue, and resting in him who has created, sustains and delights in you too. (*Pause for silent response*)

Leader: God is our Maker, Keeper and Lover.
All: **His goodness enfolds every one of his creatures and all his blessed works.**

Leader: 'For God himself is eternity, and has made us for himself alone, has restored us by his blessed Passion and keeps us in his blessed love. And all because he is goodness.'
All: **Amen.**

(27) EXPANDING CIRCLES

You will need a big sheet of paper and some felt-tip pens. On the paper draw a central circle, and four increasingly large concentric circles around it. Inside the central circle write: Ourselves. On the rim of each ring going outwards from the centre write headings that reflect widening areas of concern, e.g.: Loved Ones; Our Community; Our Country; The World.

Explain that while our prayers will start with concerns closest to us at the centre, we are going to move outwards in love and faith, as we let the Lord widen our horizons.

Start with the inmost circle and ask the group to write the names of one another inside it as a way of praying for each other. They may wish to accompany this with a simple spoken prayer addressing a specific need known to the group.

51

Now move out to the next circle. Again, invite people to write the names of loved ones within this wider ring as a prayer, alongside a short spoken prayer if appropriate. Move out in the same way to include the widening circles of community, country and world. The group could be invited to draw a symbol or simple picture to represent the prayer need if they prefer.

Finish by saying a prayer for the group to be encircled and strengthened by the Triune God:

Now may the might of God uphold us,
the love of Christ enfold us,
and the power of the Spirit embolden us this day and
evermore. Amen.

(28) CONNECTING CIRCLES

These days we no longer live in clearly defined geographical communities, but in wider networks of contact across different aspects of our lives. This exercise helps group members recognize this and develop a sense of their own individual network for personal intercession.

You will need pieces of paper and pens for each person.

Ask the group to draw a circle in the centre of their page, and write their name inside it. Explain that we all come into contact with different sets of people or networks throughout the week, e.g. in family gatherings, friendship groups, up our street, at our workplace, at the school gate or badminton club, etc. Some of these networks will overlap, or reflect areas common to all our lives; others will be unique to us.

Invite people to 'chart' their own networks by drawing other circles around their page, connected by a line to their central circle. Each circle represents a different element of their personal network. Ask them to label it – e.g. work, reading group, etc. – and allow the Spirit to bring to mind one or two in that set of people who need particular prayer. Then write these names in the appropriate circle. Give the group some minutes for this, as different networks will occur, and perhaps some surprising names will surface.

Encourage the group to reflect on what they have drawn and written. What has come out of this exercise for them?

Have a brief time of open prayer together, asking those who wish to speak out the various contact networks, and the names of people within those circles for whom they are praying. Amid so many different networks, it's important to underline the unity of the group in Christian fellowship, so it would be highly appropriate to finish by saying the Lord's Prayer or the Grace together.

Invite group members to take their network sheets home as a resource for their personal prayers for others.

(29) WARMED BY GOD'S LOVE: INTERCESSION WITH ICE CUBES

You will need a tray of ice cubes and a bowl of warm water.

Explain that the ice cubes are to represent situations and people known to us that seem hard and cold. In our prayers, we will place them into the presence of Jesus, God's living water, who alone can remove barriers and melt hearts.

Encourage the group to settle themselves, and consciously let go of any tensions and concerns that might block their attentiveness during this time of prayer.

Ask each person to bring to mind a situation that seems hard and intractable and where they feel there is no hope of breakthrough. Invite people, as they wish, to pray by speaking out the situation as they put an ice cube into the water.

After each individual prayer, ask the group to join together with the response:

Leader: Lord Jesus, Living Water,
All: **Please dissolve what we cannot resolve.**

Next, ask the group to call to mind a person they know who seems cold to God's love, or hardened to the gospel. Again invite prayer through the naming of these people alongside the placing of an ice cube in the water. This time, the group might like to affirm individual prayers with the response:

Leader: Lord Jesus, Living Water,
All: **Please melt what we cannot move.**

Conclude by focusing on the bowl of melting ice cubes, and invite people to reflect on what it says to them about the power and love of Jesus, the living water . . . About the way he works . . . About the time it takes for us to see the answers to prayer, etc. The group could either share their insights with one another, or offer them in short prayers of thanksgiving.

Keep the bowl on the table throughout the rest of the meeting, or over coffee, as a reminder that the Lord is always at work, even when nothing instant or noisy is happening.

(30) WWJS (WHAT WOULD JESUS SAY?)

You will need some recent quotes from people who have made the news: politicians, celebrities or ordinary folk who have hit the headlines in some way. Ideally, ask the group the week before to listen out for any comment that particularly strikes them. It might be something outrageous, poignant, thought-provoking or simply revealing of a particular way of looking at the world.

If it is not possible to assemble these comments from the group, you could collect your own. In either case they need to be written down so everyone can see them. You will also need a Bible.

Explain that we are going to look at what the world says, seek to discern what Jesus would say in response, and pray for the need that emerges from the difference.

Invite the group to reflect on the first comment and contribute along the lines suggested above. What do they think about this quote? How would Jesus connect with the speaker and the situation? Is there a passage from the Gospels that seems relevant? Encourage the group to be open to spiritual insights and scriptural wisdom. They might like to write down any appropriate Bible verses or responses on another piece of paper, and set it next to the original quote.

Given what the group senses Jesus would say, how might they pray in response? Invite one or two to offer short prayers in the light of what has emerged, and move on to the next comment. You could complete the exercise by placing the quotes underneath the Bible, as an act of submitting the world's words to God's words, and, most supremely, to Jesus, God's Living Word.

Note

This exercise could be adapted to become **WWJS (What Would Jesus See?)**, through the use of pictures and photographs from magazines or newspapers. Group members could bring along images that have struck them, and reflect together on what Jesus would see in the image, and how he would respond.

If there is time, you could start this exercise with the group choosing and cutting out pictures from magazines and papers brought along or provided at the meeting.

You could conclude these prayers by placing these images round the foot of the cross, the humble picture of Christ's loving reconciliation for a world that denies or distorts his image.

(31) SIGNS OF THE CROSS

You will need a large sheet of flip-chart sized paper to place in the middle of the group, plus felt pens of various colours.

You will also need a standing cross as part of this exercise.

Explain that as we see the cross shape used in many different contexts around us, we can use these to prompt our prayers of intercession. Encourage people to be open to the prayer connections the Holy Spirit might bring to mind in this activity.

Start by writing '2 + 2 = 5' on the sheet of paper and alongside it place a large red 'X'. This sort of cross means we have got something wrong. Invite whoever wishes to pray a brief prayer along the lines suggested by this type of cross: e.g. for those struggling with failure or who have wrong things in their lives that need forgiveness, etc. Then invite anyone to draw or illustrate another way in which we see the cross used, again followed by a short time of open prayers in response to whatever ideas have been triggered.

Examples of crosses might include: crossroads, a cross as a piece of jewellery, noughts and crosses, the multiplication sign, a kiss at the end of a letter, a vote, and so on.

Continue as long as the ideas last. Then place the standing cross in the middle of the sheet of paper and read Colossians 1.19, 20:

'For in Christ all the fullness of God was pleased to dwell, and through him God was pleased to reconcile to himself all things, whether in earth or in heaven, by making peace through the blood of his cross.'

Finish by spending a few moments in prayer thanking Jesus for all the Cross means to us as his followers.

(32) FIVE MINUTES THERE, FIVE MINUTES BACK

While a long prayer-walk might be an overly time-consuming activity that might exclude some, most people would be able to walk for ten minutes at their own pace.

You will need a local map of your immediate area. A site plan of your meeting place might also be useful.

Explain that we will prepare to intercede by collecting ideas through a short 'listening' prayer-walk, where we'll be open to whatever prayer need the Holy Spirit puts on our hearts through what we see, hear, touch and smell.

Invite people to walk for five minutes in any direction they choose, and then return to the room. They may even wish simply to wander slowly round the outside or inside of the building if that is appropriate to your group's meeting place. Wherever they go, they need to walk in silence, keeping their senses tuned in to what God may be saying through their surroundings. Encourage people to be open to whatever prayer connection occurs to them. Those unable to walk might like to ask God to speak through the meeting room itself as they sit and seek to look with his eyes.

When everyone has returned, spend a few moments sharing where people went and what they discerned, perhaps comparing notes by looking together at the map and site plan. Have any similar insights emerged? What might this suggest about that particular issue? Invite people to offer what has been shared in simple prayers, encouraging them to stay with the topics that seemed especially important. Finish by saying the Grace.

Reflect together on how God might prompt us to pray if we walked through our week with a similar awareness of our surroundings. Could the group agree to try this out and report back on what happens at the following meeting?

Note

This could also be done as an imaginative walk together round a familiar place such as your town centre or High Street. Use your local Visitor Information Centre or library for more detailed maps of your main street or shopping centre. Distribute these to the group, so you can refer to the route as you 'prayerwalk' the area together. Introduce a section of the walk at a time (e.g. 'We're going to walk now from the Market Square up Queen Street towards the Museum'), and invite people to imagine themselves making their way along the road. What do they see and hear that might prompt a prayer?

Encourage people to pray out loud as things occur, and be open to the Spirit's creativity. They may know particular shops and local workers, and shop-fronts themselves can suggest prayer angles: e.g. an Accessorize shop may prompt prayers for those who see Jesus as just an optional accessory to their lives, while a pet shop might remind us of our responsibility to care for God's creation.

(33) THE WRITING'S ON THE WALL

You will need a very large piece of paper, across which you have drawn oblong shapes to resemble the bricks of a wall. You may want to obtain a brick-coloured sheet from your local stationer's for this. You will also need felt-tip pens and Blu-Tack.

Attach the paper to a wall. Explain that we're going to ask the Lord to help us discern the blocks that create a dividing wall between our local community and the loving light of Christ, and pray for their removal.

Begin by reading Isaiah 2.12, 15: **'For the Lord of hosts has a day against all that is proud and lofty, against all that is lifted up and high . . . against every high tower, and against every fortified wall.'**

Ask the group to let the Holy Spirit bring to mind any 'bricks' that form a wall separating the community from Christ. As these occur, they write or draw them in one of the brick-spaces on the paper 'wall'.

Once there is plenty of writing on the wall, start praying for it to fall! Ask the group to stand facing the wall, and remind them that Scripture affirms that the walls of Jericho came down by faith (Hebrews 11.30). Invite people to offer prayers about the issues written on this wall. If preferred, they can use a simple form of words such as: **'Lord, by the power of your Spirit please remove the block of alcohol abuse'**, etc.

Complete your prayers by spending some moments praising God who has the power to bring down all barriers that oppose his rule.

End by reading Ephesians 2.14: **'Christ is our peace; in his flesh he has made both groups into one and has broken down the dividing wall, that is, the hostility between us.'** You may then wish to share the Peace together.

Note

Another Brick in the Wall represents another approach using this idea. Pass a brick round the group, and ask each person to name a block it represents as they hold it. (If nothing comes to mind, they can simply pass it on.) Then place the brick in the centre of the group, and focus on it as you offer short prayers about the issues mentioned. This does not have the same visual impact as the wall, but the brick's heaviness makes it a powerful symbol of a spiritual block.

(34) I SEE YOUR SMILE . . .

You will need to cut out and prepare a selection of photographs or magazine images of different faces. Aim for as much variety of expressions, settings, ages and nationalities as you can. The important thing is that it is possible to look into the face of each person. You will also need some background music to accompany the reflective part of this activity. An excellent choice (and the piece that inspired the creation of this exercise!) is Beth Nielsen Chapman's 'I Find Your Love', the title track from the film Calendar Girls. *This is on the film's soundtrack CD, produced by Hollywood Records 2003. If this is unavailable, reflect on the pictures you have chosen and be open to what song or piece of music your choice suggests to you.*

Arrange the images and pictures on a central table so the group can gather round them. Explain that we are going to use these to prompt our intercessions. A Christian military doctor involved in the liberation of the concentration camps after the Second World War was once asked how he managed to minister among such suffering. He replied that whenever he felt in danger of being overwhelmed, he walked the length of the camp and looked into the faces of everyone he saw, until he could see the face of Christ looking back. As we prepare to intercede, we will look into these faces, and allow the Lord to speak to us through them about how we might pray for human needs.

As you start the music, ask people to listen and to look carefully into the faces of the assembled pictures. What do they notice? What needs, aspirations, joys, griefs or hopes are there? What prayers for others does the Holy Spirit prompt in response?

As the music finishes, allow some moments for quiet, and then offer the opportunity for open prayer. Invite people to pick up a picture that has spoken to them, hold it up for all to see, and speak out the prayer it has prompted. They will need to continue holding the picture for a few moments to allow others touched by the same image to contribute their prayer.

Finish by saying the Grace together, encouraging everyone to look at the faces and into the eyes of the rest of the group as they do so.

4

Praying for one another

(35) WHERE WILL YOU BE TOMORROW?

Often we know one another's church face, but have very little idea what we all do for the rest of the week. This exercise can help overcome this, as well as being an opportunity to pray for specific situations.

Go round the group asking each one to say where he or she will be at 11.30 tomorrow morning. What will they be doing? What are their challenges and prayer needs?

Once everyone has shared, invite the group to offer brief prayers for one another, based on what they have heard. They can use their own words or, if they prefer, use a simple form of words such as '**Lord, please be with Jane with the children at home**'; '**Lord, please be with John at the office meeting**', and so on. Close by saying the Grace together.

You could also encourage people to pause to offer a short prayer for someone in the group actually at 11.30 the next morning.

(36) GODLY GROWTH

Sometimes groups become tongue-tied in sharing personal items for prayer. This exercise can help people express a prayer need in a medium other than words. It may work better with a group who know, or are getting to know, one another. The exercise could be done at the start of a Christian discipleship course and repeated at the end, to help people reflect on how their initial 'tree' has grown or changed.

You will need a visual aid – either a view of trees outside a window, an appropriate picture, or a bonsai tree placed centrally. You will also need a small standing cross – preferably of wood – and pieces of paper plus drawing/colouring materials such as crayons or felt-tip pens.

The prayer leader reads from Psalm 1.1–3:

'Happy are those ... whose delight is in the law of the Lord. They are like trees planted by streams of water, which yield their fruit in its season, and their leaves do not wither. In all that they do, they prosper.'

As you look at the tree(s) together, ask group members to say what they see. What is it about a tree that makes it such an effective picture of the healthy, mature Christian?

Possible observations might include: the tree's roots go deep to find nourishment; it endures through the seasons; it bends with the wind; its branches offer a resting place; its leaves give shade and trunk support; its flowers and fruit bring beauty and nourishment for others; each tree is unique, etc.

Ask group members to draw what sort of tree they feel they are at the moment. Then invite them in turn to place their pictures on the table by the cross (the tree on which Christ was hanged) and, if they wish, say something about what they have drawn. Where do they need and want to grow to become more fruitful 'trees'? Invite the next person to offer a short prayer on each one's behalf. If spontaneous prayer is hard for the group, you could end with the words of Psalm 1.1–3 or Jeremiah 17.7, 8 as a prayer, said individually or as a group.

(37) HELD IN THE NET

Sometimes personal prayers made in a group can be forgotten between one meeting and the next, which is a shame when many prayer concerns are of an ongoing rather than one-off nature. It's also easy to miss out on sharing how and where God has answered these prayers. Bringing a prayer-net out week by week can help everyone keep track of whether to continue praying or rejoice in the answers.

You will need a piece of garden netting and strands of coloured wool or narrow ribbons of various colours.

Place everything centrally and ask the group to call to mind a personal prayer need for themselves or someone known to them. Invite people to take a strand of wool and tie it into the net as a prayer for a particular need, saying out loud as they do so, 'This is a prayer for . . .' They might also wish to take a strand of the same coloured wool home with them, to tuck in a Bible or place on a bedside table as a reminder of the prayer they have made. The net can be brought out in subsequent meetings and updated: more wool can be added, and the group invited to share what has happened regarding the prayers represented by the strands already there.

You may wish in later weeks to ask people to untie or cut off the strands representing prayers that have been answered – whether with a 'yes', 'no' or 'not yet' – along with some simple words of thanksgiving. This can encourage the group to continue to pray for themselves and one another.

(38) THINKING OF YOU

You will need a selection of picture postcards, plus pens. Your cards could be traditional holiday-style postcards with views, but you could also incorporate others, e.g. cards from an art gallery or museum, or free advertising postcards from your local coffee shop or gym. Whatever your sources, ensure you have a good range of pictures and/or designs on display, as you set the cards out in the middle of the group.

Explain that when we go away, on holiday or elsewhere, we often send postcards to let family and friends know we're thinking of them. In this exercise we will write and send a 'prayer postcard' to let another group member know we're praying for him or her. Paul's epistles often open with his prayers for the believers he is writing to, as an expression of encouragement and support. Though Paul writes at greater length, shorter prayers can be just as effective; receiving a postcard can mean as much as getting a letter.

Ask the group to work in pairs, and take it in turns to tell their partner about a personal prayer need they feel able to share.

Next, ask them to choose an appropriate postcard to 'send' to their partner. On it, they write the person's name, and a postcard-length prayer in response to what has been shared. Pairs then send their cards to one another by taking turns to read the prayer each has written, in the presence of the partner, and giving him or her the postcard.

Encourage people to put their cards up at home – perhaps on their fridge or mantelpiece – as a reminder of the prayer offered for them.

Note

This idea could also be used for personal prayers. Group members choose the card they feel appropriate for them, and write their own prayer on it. The cards can then be posted to Jesus by being read out or simply placed in silence at the foot of a cross or lighted candle.

(39) HIGHWAY CODE PRAYERS

You could shorten this exercise by cutting out paper road sign shapes beforehand. However, a shared craft activity often brings people together in itself and so forms a valuable lead-in to group prayer.

You will need copies of the Highway Code road signs, plain paper, felt-tip pens, scissors, rulers and a drawing compass. You will also need a long grey scarf or something similar to represent a road, and a cross or large white candle for Christ.

Place the 'road' in the middle of the group, with the cross or candle at one end.

Explain that just as road signs inform, direct and warn us as we drive so that we find our way clearly and travel safely, so we need God's directions, guidance and help as we journey closer to Christ.

Invite each member of the group to spend some time reflecting on the different Highway Code road signs, and select the one they sense most represents a current prayer need. For example:

Roundabout: 'I feel I'm going round in circles.'
Speed limit: 'I know I need the gift of patience.'

No left turn:	'I'm being tempted to go the wrong way.'
Crossroads/Junction:	'I've got a decision to make', etc.

As people select a suitable symbol, they make their own copy of it, using the materials provided.

Once everyone has done this, ask each person in turn to place his or her sign somewhere along the road leading to the cross, and say something about why it was chosen. No one need feel under pressure to open up in any great depth or detail: God knows the full meaning of the sign for each one. As each person places a sign, pause for a few moments, inviting anyone who wishes to offer a short prayer out loud, based on what has been shared.

If you are able to, you may wish to keep the road, signs and cross out in the room as an opening activity for the following week. Have any of the group's prayers been answered? Are they further along the road than last time? Would they like to move their road sign closer to the cross – or even change it – as a result?

(40) A PRAYERFUL TOUCH

You may find some gentle background music helpful for this exercise. A symbol of Christ, such as a lighted candle or cross placed in the middle of the group, would also help form a united focus.

Ask the group to form a circle and join hands. Explain that you are going to pray silently for one another, going round the circle one by one. Encourage the whole group to continue to 'hold' the person being prayed for in the presence of Christ, even when it is not their turn to pray. It may be that the Lord brings to mind a particular insight, encouragement, or word of Scripture for that person that can be sensitively shared with them afterwards individually.

Invite the first one to be prayed for to share a prayer need briefly, if he or she wishes. Otherwise, group members can offer whatever prayers are on their hearts for that person.

Ask the group to close their eyes, and for the one being prayed for to squeeze the hand of the person on the right. That person then prays a silent prayer for him or her. The person praying, on finishing, squeezes the hand of the next person on the right, who prays his or her prayer, passing it on by a squeeze of the hand to the next person, and so on round the room.

The last one to pray closes by saying '**Amen**' out loud, to indicate that the prayer circle is complete. Then go on to the next person in the circle and repeat the process. Finish by saying the Grace together. If appropriate, you may wish to invite feedback on what it felt like to be prayed for in this way.

(41) PART OF THE BODY

This exercise works best with a group who know one another reasonably well. It can be a very encouraging activity. People are often amazed that qualities they see as just ordinary and natural to them are recognized by others as special gifts. This can give them a new appreciation of what they contribute to the wider group.

You will need a fairly large, simple, paper figure of a person cut up into separate body parts, sufficient for each member of the group to be given one. You will also need pens.

Give out a different body part to each person, and introduce the activity by reading 1 Corinthians 12.12–26. Remind the group that every member is a unique part of the body of Christ with a special contribution to make.

Everyone now writes their name on the part they've been given and, alongside it, a gift (ability, quality or talent) they offer to the wider group. The parts are then all passed round between everyone. Each group member writes on each of the other parts a gift he or she recognizes and values in that person. It doesn't matter if the same gift is recognized more than once.

Once everyone has written something on each part, including their own, pass them back to their owners and give people some moments to read and reflect on what has been written. Are there any surprises? Are any gifts underlined by being affirmed more than once? Now ask people to assemble the parts to make a complete figure. Look at this figure together. What range of gifts emerges? Do these balance one another?

Turn to prayer by re-reading 1 Corinthians 12.12 and inviting people to give thanks to Christ for one another and the different gifts they bring. Encourage people to offer prayers for the body of Christ to find ways for the different parts to work together and not tear itself apart.

Express unity at the end by praying the Lord's Prayer as one body.

(42) GETTING CONNECTED

You will need two very large sheets of paper – preferably flip-chart size – and different coloured marker pens.

Place the sheets in the middle of the group. At the top of both, write 'God', and at the bottom write 'Jesus'. Draw a long line from Jesus up to God, with an arrowhead at the top of it.

Explain that this represents the direct line Jesus had to God as he prayed to his Father during his earthly life. But sometimes when we aim our prayers to God, our line from earth to heaven does not seem so connected.

Invite people to reflect on this and, in their own time, write their name somewhere on the first sheet of paper, and above it draw a line that they feel represents their prayers for a particular issue or need on their heart at the moment. They can do this without actually revealing the specific need if they prefer. One or two may feel their prayers are getting straight through to God, for which give thanks. Others might be finding things less straightforward.

If people are struggling to depict what they feel is happening, some possible prayer lines might be:

A circle: for prayers going round and round, getting nowhere

A wavy line: for when we started to pray, but lost the momentum

An arrow with a box shape above it: for prayer that seems to be hitting a block

A tangled line: for when prayer feels confused

A zigzag line: for when we're finding it hard to be 'straight' with God

Once people have drawn their lines, invite people to pray 'one-line' prayers for one another that the Spirit will straighten and empower their prayers, and enable them to know they're connected to the God who always responds.

For this part of the exercise, use the second sheet. As each person prays for another, he or she writes that group member's name on this sheet and draws a long arrow line connecting it straight to God.

Having ensured that all have been prayed for, finish by saying the Lord's Prayer together, the prayer Jesus himself taught his disciples when they asked him how to pray.

(43) WATCH AND PRAY

Having something to watch as we pray can help people overcome self-consciousness, as well as acting as a visual symbol of the Spirit of God at work in the one being prayed for.

You will need a sealable bottle, some baby oil, water and food colouring. The peaceful colours of blue or green would be particularly appropriate.

Pour water and some food colouring into the bottle, add baby oil and seal it up.

You will also need a selection of appropriate peace-giving words of Jesus, plus a concluding blessing or prayer printed on a sheet of paper with enough copies for everyone to see. Possible words of Jesus could include:

Your faith has saved you. Go in peace. (Luke 7.50)
Peace I leave with you. Peace I give you. (John 14.27)
Come unto me, all you that are weary and are carrying heavy burdens, and I will give you rest. (Matthew 11.28)
Do not let your hearts be troubled. Believe in God, believe also in me. (John 14.1)
Remember I am with you always, to the end of the age. (Matthew 28.20)
Even the hairs of your head are counted. So do not be afraid. (Matthew 10.30, 31)

A suggested blessing is incorporated below.

Introduce this activity by explaining how, when we're troubled by anxiety about particular situations, the resulting inner turmoil can leave us feeling confused and thoroughly 'mixed up'. Illustrate this by shaking the bottle and seeing how the two liquids combine. But as we receive Christ's peace, we gradually become still, able to separate out our priorities and gain a clearer insight into how to respond. We see a picture of this in the way the liquids progressively settle into two separate layers, with the clear oil floating on top of the coloured water. In this prayer activity the bottle will be a visual focus as we ask for Christ's peace for one another in situations that make us anxious or agitated.

Place the bottle in the middle of a central table and distribute the copies of the Bible verses. Start the prayer time by inviting whoever wishes to shake the bottle and mix the ingredients, to represent a personal issue currently causing some inner turbulence. He or she can name or briefly describe the situation, or simply shake the bottle in silence if preferred. The group then focuses on the separating liquids as they offer short prayers for the one in need. While these may include prayers about the actual situation, it's particularly important to pray for Christ's peace for the person concerned.

The group continues in prayer until the liquids have settled into clear layers. Then invite anyone to choose whichever Bible verse from the sheet he or she feels to be especially appropriate for the one being prayed for, and read it to that person. A form of words could be something like: '**Andrew, the Lord says to you, "Peace I leave with you. Peace I give you"**', etc.

The next person who wants to receive prayer starts the process again by shaking the bottle, and so on until all who wish have had the opportunity to be prayed for.

Finish by reading together the concluding blessing prayer on the sheet:

May the peace of God the Father hold us in his care.
May the peace of Jesus the Son reconcile us in his love.
May the peace of the Holy Spirit comfort us by his presence.
  Amen.

(44) MUSICAL PRAYERS

*While Paul urges Christians to 'sing psalms and hymns and
spiritual songs among yourselves' (Ephesians 5.19), singing in
a small group can feel a poor second to the sound of a church
congregation with full musical accompaniment. However,
interspersing prayers with simple unaccompanied refrains or
chants can be effective in the smaller setting, and encourage
the more reluctant singers. It also avoids the fuss of organizing
instruments. Such singing is an alternative to rather than a
pale imitation of a Sunday service. You may wish to draw
on the talents of a musically gifted group member for this. If
leading unaccompanied singing, ensure you pitch the first note
carefully. As a general rule, start the singing a tone or two
above the note you first think of. It's all too easy to err on the
side of caution by starting too low, and end up with everyone
growling into their boots by the second line. If you're not
confident of teaching a chant, play it on a CD or tape and
get people to sing along.*

---

*You will need a small basket or dish, plus pieces of paper and pens
for everyone.*

  *You will also need to teach a simple chant to the group to use in
the prayer time. Either 'O Lord, hear my prayer', from the Taizé
Community, or 'Listen, Lord', from the Iona Community's Wild
Goose Worship Group would be good choices.*

  *Word copies of your chosen chant on slips of paper could also be
helpful.*

Explain that we will offer prayers in spoken word and in song as we intercede for one another. Teach the chant to the group and ensure they have word copies if they need them. Pass round paper and pens and ask everyone to write down a personal prayer need (plus their name) on their piece of paper, fold it up and place it in the basket.

Open the prayer time by passing the basket to the first person in the group, who picks out a prayer need from it. (Anyone who selects their own should put it back and start again.) This person then offers a short prayer for the need on the paper. The whole group follows this prayer by singing the chant through together to affirm what has been spoken.

Move on to the next person and continue alternating spoken and sung prayer in this way round the whole group. The activity is completed when all have prayed and the chant has been sung together for the final time.

(45) CALLED BY NAME

This activity is particularly effective at the beginning of a group's life, as it will help members quickly become familiar with one another's names.

Find the relevant name meanings in a book or on the website <www.behindthename.com>, which also includes a list of biblical names.

You will need a list of the meanings of the names of everyone in your group.

You will also need a large sheet of flip-chart sized paper, plus felt-tip pens. Write everyone's names in a column down the left-hand side of the paper. If two people share the same name, write it down twice, so every person is individually represented.

Explain that in the Bible names are more than mere labels. Names matter to God: the Baptist's parents Zechariah and Elizabeth were *instructed* to name their son John. They may denote a position: Jacob named his last-born Benjamin – 'the son of my right hand'. They may reflect a relationship, as in Elizabeth – 'consecrated to God'. They may be given as a name to grow into: Stephen/Stephanie means 'crowned one' – the wearer of the laurel wreath of victory.

Gather the meanings of the names represented in your group, either from the people themselves or from your reference list. As you go round, write the meanings against their names on the sheet of paper, but also ask each person to add anything they wish about what their name means to them personally: e.g. they may be named after a family member or a famous character, biblical or otherwise. They may have strong feelings about their name and how it is used. Does it get shortened, for example? How do they like to be known?

Now turn to prayer. Open by reading Isaiah 43.1b: **'Do not fear, for I have redeemed you; I have called you by name, you are mine.'**

Now invite people to offer short prayers for one another, linked to the person's name. This may involve more creativity in some cases than in others. Examples of prayers might be: 'Lord, as Keith means "from the forest", so we pray for your gift of discernment for Keith. May he never miss the wood for the trees'; 'Lord, as Hilary means "cheerful one", so we pray that Hilary will know your joy day by day.'

Once everyone has been prayed for, finish by thanking God for Jesus, in whose name we pray, and reading from Philippians 2.9–11:

'. . . God highly exalted him and gave him the name that is above every other name, so that at the name of Jesus, every

knee should bend, in heaven and on earth and under the earth, and every tongue should confess that Jesus Christ is Lord, to the glory of God the Father. Amen.'

(46) FREE TO SERVE, LINKED IN LOVE

You will need a length of metal chain, easily obtainable from your local DIY store.

You may also need a large card on which is copied John 8.36: 'So if the Son makes you free, you will be free indeed.'

Explain that as Christ has set us free, we're going to ask for this to be a reality in our lives as we pray for one another. Ask the first person to pick up the chains and put them round the wrists of the next person. The chained person then brings to mind an area or aspect of life where he or she wants to be set free by Christ. He or she indicates having thought of this either by naming it out loud or just by giving the nod.

The one who placed the chains on the person then removes them with a prayer such as:

'Lord, your Word says, "If the Son makes you free, you shall be free indeed." So we ask you to release Andy from whatever binds him.'

Repeat the process round the group until all have been prayed for.

Though we've been set free from things that chain us down, as Christians we are linked into a different sort of chain, one of love and fellowship that unites and strengthens us. So end by asking everyone to cross arms and link hands (as if to sing Auld Lang Syne!), and say the Lord's Prayer together as an expression of being joined into the one Christian family.

5

Time to reflect

(47) OUT IN THE GARDEN

*On hot summer days, children often ask their teachers if they
can have their lesson outside. Perhaps we wish we could ask
for the same thing at church! This activity forms a change from
an indoor meeting during the summer, though it does depend
on there being a garden or suitable grounds readily accessible.*

Remind people of how the Bible includes gardens as places of
encounter with God: the Garden of Eden; the walled garden in
the Song of Solomon; the Garden of Gethsemane. On Easter
Day, Mary Magdalene even mistook Jesus for the gardener!

Invite people to go out into the garden and silently watch
and walk with this in mind. Encourage them to use their senses,
to touch and smell, to look and listen for how God might be
speaking through his creation; and simply to give God their
quiet attention in the garden space.

Agree a time for this, and ask people to gather back inside
towards the end of it. If appropriate, they can bring something
from the garden back in with them. Invite people to share
what happened in that time for them. You may wish to conclude by having a short time of prayer together, where these
insights and experiences can be turned into prayers of thanksgiving.

(48) WATER REFLECTION

Water is a powerful symbol, particularly so for Jesus, the living water.

This exercise needs to be approached with sensitivity. People may see difficult things 'upstream' and need some gentle pastoral support afterwards.

On a lighter practical note, concentration will be greatly improved if this exercise is done before rather than after serving coffee, for obvious reasons!

You will need a CD with the sound of running water as a background to this exercise. A central visual stimulus, such as a bowl of water with three floating candles, can also form a useful focus to lead into and out of the prayer time.

The prayer leader lights the candles, to help people settle into prayerfulness, then starts the sound of the running water.

The prayer leader guides the meditation

Allow yourselves to become still as you listen to the water . . . and imagine yourself by a cool stream in the heat and dust of a blazing day . . . As you stand on the bank you choose to step into the stream to refresh yourself . . . You wade in and feel the coolness and movement of the water against your body . . . refreshing . . . renewing . . . sparkling and alive . . . Jesus says, 'Whoever believes in me, streams of living water will flow from within him' . . . Stand in the stream and let his living water flow round you and through you . . . refreshing . . . renewing . . . washing you clear of the clutter of concerns that can clog you up inside . . . Allow the fullness of the Holy Spirit to wash you through and open you up to the presence of Christ . . .

Turn now, so you are facing downstream . . . You may be carrying things you need to let go of . . . blocks and burdens that weigh you down . . . things you are holding on to too tightly . . . Become aware of what you need to release for Jesus, the living water, to carry away . . . Let go of these things, and watch them float off down the stream . . . and feel the lightness you are left with as a result . . . Become aware again of the living water flowing round and through you, coursing into those places now freed to receive him, and let his life in . . .

Now turn yourself round to face upstream, with the water flowing towards you . . . Even as the living water bears things away, it brings other things towards you . . . gifts and challenges . . . Look upstream . . . What do you see coming towards you, borne along by the water? . . . Are there things you need to let float by, or catch hold of and receive? . . . Ask Jesus to show you what he wants you to see and how to respond . . .

The best way to prepare for what the Lord has in store is to receive him in the present . . . so continue to allow his living water to refresh, uphold, cleanse and renew you right now . . . Let the presence of Jesus, the living water, flow round and through you . . . Jesus says, 'Whoever believes in me, streams of living water will flow from within him' . . .

Now, in your own time, imagine yourself walking up out of the stream and sitting on the bank . . . and when you are ready, open your eyes and become aware of the bowl and the candles and this room around you . . .

(49) FILLING THE EMPTINESS

This exercise combines a personal response to Christ with a non-intrusive way of praying for one another. It is important

that the leader discreetly ensures no one is left out in the final
part of the exercise, as well as being pastorally aware and
available afterwards for anyone who might have found difficult
issues surfacing.

---

*You will need a jug of water. Place around it enough cups for every-
one in the group.*

The prayer leader guides the meditation

Settle yourselves into a relaxed, but alert, posture . . . You
may wish to close your eyes as the prayer continues, but for
the moment, allow your gaze to rest on one of the empty
cups . . . Think about emptiness, the emptiness of this cup
. . . What is it like to feel empty? . . . Can you recall times
when you have felt empty? Perhaps this is how you feel
now . . . It can be difficult to sense a space inside us. We're
tempted to fill it with all sorts of things, to soothe the dis-
comfort – food, drink, hobbies, work, sport, spending . . .
What are you tempted to fill your inner space with? Let Jesus
show you . . . Offer that area to him, so he can set you free
from any compulsion to consume for comfort . . . Jesus says,
'Blessed are the poor in Spirit, for theirs is the kingdom of
heaven' . . . So we need not be afraid of acknowledging our
emptiness . . . If we stay with our emptiness, we begin to be
aware of what it is we really need, instead of feverishly filling
ourselves with a substitute that cannot truly satisfy . . . If we
stay with our emptiness, we have space to receive what Jesus
has to give instead of greedily grabbing ourselves a quick
fix . . . If we rush to fill ourselves up, we can lose touch with
our deepest desires and needs, and miss out on the fullness
of the kingdom of heaven . . . Take a few moments to allow

Jesus to bring to the surface what it is you truly long for in your times of greatest emptiness . . . Love? . . . Acceptance? . . . Peace? . . . Forgiveness? . . . In the quiet, bring this desire to Jesus now, for only he can truly satisfy it . . . Jesus says, 'Those who drink of the water I will give them will never be thirsty. The water that I will give will become in them a spring of water, gushing up to eternal life' . . .

When you are ready, take a cup, pour in water from the jug, and give it to another person in the group, for we cannot fill ourselves . . . As you offer the water, pray that Jesus will pour his fullness into empty places . . . As you receive the water and drink, imagine the fullness of Jesus reaching down into your deepest being, and making you whole . . . As those who drink from the water of life together, let us bless one another in the words of the Grace . . .

(50) I AM WITH YOU ALWAYS

This exercise challenges us to become aware that Christ is with us wherever we are, and allows him to show us how he is present in places where we find it hard to recognize him. The opportunity to share insights afterwards can highlight situations where group members can pray supportively for one another.

Explain that, though Jesus promises to be with us always, we're often more aware of him in some places than others. In this reflective meditation, we will focus on his presence in two contrasting areas of our lives.

The prayer leader guides the reflection
Settle into a posture that is relaxed, but enables you to stay alert and attentive . . . Close your eyes . . . Become aware of your breathing and allow it to become gentle . . . quiet

. . . rhythmic . . . in and out . . . Jesus promises, 'I am with you always . . .' We all have particular places where we naturally feel a sense of God's presence . . . Perhaps in the city, or the country, or by the sea . . . in a majestic church building or in a warm home . . . Wherever it is for you, picture that place now, and see yourself going into it . . . Take a moment to imagine it fully . . . the sights . . . sounds . . . smells . . . the atmosphere . . . What is it like to be there? . . . As you rest in this place, imagine Jesus coming into the scene, to meet you . . . How does it feel to see him approach? . . . Welcome him . . . Tell Jesus what this place means to you . . . and listen for his reply . . . Enjoy being with him here for a few moments . . .

It's time to go now, so say your farewells to Jesus . . . and walk out of this place . . . You're on your way to somewhere else . . . Jesus promises, 'I am with you always', but we all find ourselves in places where it seems as though God is absent. . . . Where do you find it especially hard to sense God's presence? . . . Picture that place now, and see yourself going into it . . . Take a moment to imagine it fully . . . the sights . . . sounds . . . smells . . . the atmosphere . . . What is it like to be there? . . . As you stay in this place, imagine Jesus coming into the scene to meet you . . . How does it feel to see him approach? . . . Welcome him . . . Tell Jesus what this place means to you . . . and listen for his reply . . . Is there something he wants to show you? . . . Stay with him here for a few moments . . .

It's time to leave this place now, so say your farewells to Jesus . . . and walk away . . . but Jesus promises, 'I am with you always', and so as you come back to this place, right now, he is here again, in the midst of us . . . Take a moment to come back into this room, and when you are ready, open your eyes.

Conclude this exercise by inviting people to share insights they have gained, if they wish. How did their experience of being with Jesus in these two places compare? Did they see anything new about how he is always with them? What difference might this make to going into these places in the future? How can we pray for one another in difficult places?

(51) SCENT FROM GOD

You will need a selection of things that produce fragrant or attractive smells, e.g. bath or aromatherapy oils, pot-pourri, flowers, soap, perfume, spices, herbs, ground coffee, etc. Place these in the middle of the group.

You will also need an oil burner with fragrant oil.

Some gentle background music for the prayer itself could be helpful – e.g. the playing of 'May the fragrance of Jesus fill this place', or 'Let our praise to you be as incense'.

Invite the group to spend some time sampling the various fragrances set out in front of them. Which do they prefer? What is it like to breathe in a beautiful scent?

Explain how in the book of Revelation (8.3, 4), incense was offered on the altar so that its rising smoke mingled with the prayers of the saints before God's throne. Our prayers are a pleasing fragrance to the Lord who delights to savour our response to him. We represent this by lighting the oil burner to open our prayer time.

In Ephesians (5.2) Paul describes Jesus' love and self-giving for us as a 'fragrant offering and sacrifice to God'. Invite people to offer simple prayers of thanksgiving for Jesus and all he has done for us.

Paul tells the Corinthian church that God uses us to spread far and wide the fragrance that comes from knowing Christ. We ourselves become the aroma of Christ in God's purposes (2 Corinthians 2.14, 15). Who have we known whose presence has been like a breath of something beautiful for God in our lives? Ask people to name those who've been the fragrance of Christ to them in short prayers of thanksgiving.

We too are called to bring the aroma of Christ to those for whom life smells rotten or rancid. We take Christ's life into ourselves and exude his fragrance to others as we live for him. Invite people, in their own time, to pick up and smell the fragrance of their choice, and breathe it in slowly and deeply, as a prayer of receiving Christ – an unseen but powerful presence – and of asking him to enable them to be truly a 'Scent from God' for those around them day by day.

Read 2 Corinthians 2.14 together as a final prayer: '**But thanks be to God, who in Christ always leads us in triumphal procession, and through us spreads in every place the fragrance that comes from knowing him.**' Amen.

(52) TASTE AND SEE

You will need a large assortment of wrapped chocolates, placed on a tray in the middle of the group, along with the key from their box identifying what the different chocolates are.

Gentle music could also form a helpful background as people reflect and respond.

Explain that we're going to respond to the encouragement in Psalm 34 to 'taste and see that the Lord is good', by using the chocolates as a focus for our personal prayers.

Invite the group to settle into quiet as the music begins, and read aloud Psalm 34.8–10, as a reminder of the Lord's faithfulness in providing for our every need. As they reflect silently on the 'good things' the Lord gives, ask people to come forward when they are ready and make their prayer response by selecting the chocolate they sense is most appropriate to them personally at this time. Allow people to take their time, and encourage them to be open to the Spirit's prompting as they make their choice.

(The possibilities are wide here: people may identify with being a hard nut or soft-centred, and want the Lord's inner transformation; a toffee may represent a particularly sticky situation they're chewing over in prayer; it may be the chocolate's appearance that speaks – a triangular-shaped one for the Trinity, or a brightly wrapped one for someone who wants to show their colours for Christ, etc.)

When all have chosen, invite everyone to unwrap and eat their chocolate, to 'taste and see that the Lord is good', as they offer their own personal prayer in their hearts. Encourage people to savour the chocolate's taste and sweetness, and imagine taking in the sweetness of Jesus as he comes and meets them at their point of need.

Conclude by reading Psalm 34.1–3, and encourage people to offer brief prayers of praise and thanksgiving to the Lord who provides for us so generously.

(53) FACE UP TO GOD

This exercise will work best with a group who are coming to know one another. Done sensitively, it can be a powerful reminder of God's total acceptance of every aspect of us – a truth that can so easily slip away from our awareness.

You will need enough paper plates for each member of the group, plus pens and felt-tip pens.

Give everyone a paper plate, and on it ask them to represent the face they show to the world. They can do this in any way they like: by drawing a face; writing a slogan that sums up how they are to other people, or by using different words, shapes, symbols and colours to convey who they are to others.

Next ask people to turn their plates over and on the other side to represent aspects of the person they feel they are *inside*, the things that others don't see behind the face they wear for those around them. How different will this be?

Ask the group to work in pairs, showing their partner their plate's 'public face', and explaining what they have depicted. Does this fit the picture their partner has of them? Now ask the pairs to talk about what's on the reverse side of their plates. They need not actually show this side to their partners, or even reveal everything on it if they do not wish, but encourage people to share what they dare and allow their partner to respond. What does it feel like to do this?

Now turn to prayer. Ask everyone to settle themselves with their plate placed on their lap, 'public face' up to God. It's important for all to close their eyes for this exercise, so people can be comfortable about the privacy of what's on their plate.

The prayer leader guides the reflective response

Think about the face you present to the world . . . And for a moment, reflect upon the face you present to God . . . How do you want him to see you? . . .

Read Psalm 139.1–6 (*Pause*)

God sees behind the mask and through appearances . . . So now turn your plate over, so that you allow what is behind the mask to be face up to God . . . What does it feel like to expose to him the person you know yourself to be inside? . . .

Read Psalm 139.7–12 (*Pause*)

God brings light into our dark places . . . He knows who we are inside and out, and does not judge us . . . We can dare to reveal ourselves to him because he loves us . . . Now put the whole plate under your chair on the floor, and sit in God's presence with nothing on your lap apart from empty, open hands . . . God knows the real you, behind your image and beyond your knowledge . . . How does it feel to be a completely open book to him? . . .

Read Psalm 139.13–18 (*Pause*)

God knows everything about us, past, present and future . . . He knows everything about us, public, private and undiscovered . . .

And so we rest our whole being in the God who has formed us, the Son who has redeemed us, and the Spirit who sustains us . . . Amen.

(54) IN WEAKNESS AND IN STRENGTH

Although the reflection is guided towards a general response, individuals may experience it in quite different ways. Some may recognize and take delight in the creative potential of their 'less preferred' hand. Opportunity for feedback afterwards could yield some rich insights.

You will need sheets of paper and drawing materials such as pens, pencils and crayons.

Give a sheet of paper to each person and ask everyone to draw a line down the middle of it. On one half, they are to draw and colour a simple picture or image. Once they've finished, they repeat the process on the other half of the sheet, but this time using their other hand. People may opt to copy what they've drawn already, or perhaps try something completely different.

As people produce their pictures, encourage them to talk about their experience, particularly the contrast between working with their preferred hand and their less preferred one. What thoughts and feelings are they aware of as they draw with the 'wrong' hand? How do they view the results of their different efforts? Ask people to bear these experiences in mind as they turn to a prayer response.

The prayer leader guides the reflection

As we move from action to reflection, let yourselves become settled and relaxed . . . Have your pictures on your lap in front of you, to use as a focus for your attention . . . Look at what you've created with the hand you prefer to use . . . How do you see it? . . . What feelings or thoughts emerged as you drew with that hand? . . . Can you link these to how you approach other activities in your life? . . . Using what comes naturally can make us feel confident . . . able . . . in control . . . Thank the Lord for the activities and abilities that come naturally to you . . . Yet all our resources ultimately come from God alone . . . St Paul urges us to 'be strong in the grace that is in Christ Jesus' . . . And so offer to the Lord all your natural strengths, that you may stay mindful that everything is a gift from him . . . Invite Jesus to be Lord of all you do in response to his call upon these abilities, that he may direct what he has given for his purposes . . .

Now look at what you've created with the hand you prefer not to use . . . How do you see this picture? . . . What feelings or thoughts emerged as you drew with this other hand? . . . Can you link these to how you approach other activities in your life? . . . Using what does not come so naturally can make us feel awkward . . . clumsy . . . not in control . . . And there may be things we avoid doing because of this . . . If that is so for you, bring these things into the Lord's presence, and thank him, even for them . . . For God can meet us powerfully where we know we cannot rely on our own resources . . . St Paul reminds us that God's grace is sufficient, for his 'power is made perfect in weakness' . . . And so offer to the Lord those activities you avoid or feel reluctant to do through a sense of your own natural weaknesses . . . Offer your willingness to respond where the Lord calls you into areas that expose your personal limitations, and invite him to be your strength . . . Now hold both pictures in your attention . . . Thank the Lord for *all* he has made you and for *all* you create for him . . . Ask him to breathe through the whole picture, so that whatever you do, the Creator's hand will be around yours to strengthen and empower . . . to guide and steady . . . As we come to the end, write a short thank-you prayer for something that has come out of this reflection time . . . Use whichever hand you wish, but write across both halves of the page.

(55) GOD BE IN MY EYES

You will need a painting or poster that all can gather round and look at together.

Explain that we are going to look at this picture and allow the Lord to speak to us through it, and that we'll prepare for this by settling into a receptive frame of mind. Ask people to close their eyes, relax, consciously let go of any concerns or pre-occupations, and to be open to whatever the Lord wants to show them. Ask people to gently tune into their relationship with God, and become aware of what he means to them right now.

Help the group move into this quietness by reading the prayer 'God be in my head':

God be in my head, and in my understanding;
God be in my eyes and in my looking;
God be in my mouth and in my speaking;
God be in my heart and in my thinking;
God be at mine end and at my departing.

Invite people to gather round the painting and look at it. Encourage them to gaze calmly over the whole picture, and be receptive to the Spirit drawing their attention to particular colours, shapes, textures, figures or areas or aspects of it.

After a suitable time, ask people to stay with whatever things have caught their attention, and hold them openly before God. What feelings, thoughts and longings do they find arising in response as they do so? These may point to some aspect of God, or shed light on some area of people's relationship with him that is personally relevant. Allow people time to continue to gaze and make their own prayer response in the quiet.

Begin to draw things to a close by inviting people, when they're ready, to shift their attention out from the one focus that they've been praying around, and view the painting as a whole. Finally, ask people to widen their focus even further by becoming aware of the group around the painting – each one a work of art created by God in whose image we've been made.

Close the time by thanking the Lord for all he has made, and saying the Grace together as a way of affirming one another as God's artwork.

Dependent on the group, it can be very fruitful for people to share what they have seen in and through the picture, as far as they are willing. Hearing what are often widely different responses to the same stimulus can be amazing in itself – and might even prompt further prayers of thanksgiving and intercession for one another!

(56) READ, REFLECT, RESPOND, REST

This activity introduces the traditional form of Bible-based prayer called Lectio Divina. *While we often skim-read and rush to get to the end of a passage, this approach enables us to make unhurried space to meet God in his word and allow it to touch our spirits and transform our lives more deeply.*

Lectio Divina *is essentially an individual practice, but by guiding a group in* Lectio Divina, *you may open up a way of reading the Bible that people can continue by themselves. It can be a great help to have someone guide us through such a process and 'hold' the different stages for us, so we can focus fully on the exercise itself.*

Don't rush this activity. The silences should not be less than a minute! Gauge an appropriate length by taking part in the activity yourself, as much as you're able.

You will need to choose a short Bible passage, e.g. Joshua 1.5–9, Psalm 23, Isaiah 43.1–7, Zephaniah 3.14–20, John 1.1–18, 1 Corinthians 13.1–7. A Gospel passage where Jesus is teaching works better than one where he is interacting with others. (See suggestion 79 for a more appropriate prayer approach to the latter.)

Explain that we are going to have some Bible-based prayer using a centuries-old practice known as *Lectio Divina*, or 'divine reading'. This way of engaging with Scripture follows four stages:

Lectio:	Reading and letting a particular phrase or word from the passage strike us.
Meditatio:	Reflecting on what emerges from this phrase for us.
Oratio:	Responding in prayers that arise from our reflections.
Contemplatio:	Resting in the word and presence of the Lord.

Explain that you will guide people through these stages through repeated readings of the passage. They're not to worry if they lag behind in hearing their phrase or find that reflecting and responding start to overlap. This way of praying has its own natural rhythm. People need not feel pressured to listen to every part of the passage at each reading; where the Lord has underlined a particular phrase, they can stay with it in prayer and let the rest of the reading wash over them.

Also explain that in some early monastic traditions, before the days of personal Bibles, the community would gather to listen to the day's passage being read. (This would be read slowly again and again, and when a monk had heard the word particularly for him, he would leave and return to his cell to reflect on it. For the purposes of this exercise, however, we will stay in the room.)

The prayer leader guides the Lectio Divina

Position yourselves so you are comfortably seated, but alert and attentive. Allow your breathing to become settled and rhythmic. Prepare yourself to listen with your whole being to the Word of God for you today.

As you listen to the **reading**, be open to the Spirit catching your attention with a particular word or phrase. And let it stay with you in the silence.

Read Isaiah 43.1–7 for the first time.

(*Silence*)

Stay with your word or phrase, and if you wish, quietly speak it out loud.

(*Pause*)

As you listen to the reading again, be open to the **reflections**, thoughts and feelings that your particular word or phrase prompts in you. Gently muse and mull over what arises in God's presence. And let it resonate with you in the silence.

Read Isaiah 43.1–7 for the second time.

(*Silence*)

As you reflect, let your reflections crystallize into the key insights, the central feelings that have emerged for you.

(*Pause*)

As you listen to the reading again, be open to the personal prayers that arise in you in **response** to these reflections – even those prayers beyond words. And let them be expressed to the Lord in the silence.

Read Isaiah 43:1–7 for the third time.

(*Silence*)

As you respond, if you wish to give voice to any prayers, quietly speak them out loud.

(*Pause*)

As you listen to the reading for the last time, allow your whole self to **rest** in the presence of the Living Word. No more doing, just being in quiet surrender to him in the silence.
Read Isaiah 43.1–7 for the fourth time.
(*Silence*)

Lord, we thank you that your word always accomplishes the purpose for which you intend it. Make your word to us this day fully fruitful for you in your time and way. Amen.

Give some opportunity for people to share their experiences of this exercise, which may vary from fulfilling to frustrating. Could they see themselves using this approach in their personal Bible reading?

(57) REFLECTING ON RUBBISH

Usually we focus our attention on objects of beauty, but what might God say to us and about us through what we discard rather than what we want to keep?

You will need some rubbish! You might want to don rubber gloves and collect from your local neighbourhood, or dive into your waste bins at home. Arrange the rubbish on a tray, and in the middle place a representation of Christ, either a cross or a tall white candle. Place this unusual – and perhaps less than fragrant – collection on a central table.

Some gentle background music might be helpful for this reflection.

Explain that we are going to ask God to speak to us through what we do not usually consider of much value: what we, or those around us, have thrown away.

Start the music, light the candle if you are using it, and invite people to gaze at the display (and pick something up from it if they wish).

Read the following verses as an aid to further focus the group at the beginning of the reflection time:

Isaiah 53.2, 3 '. . . he had no form or majesty that we should look at him, nothing in his appearance that we should desire him. He was despised and rejected by others . . . one from whom others hide their faces. He was despised, and we held him of no account.'

1 Corinthians 1.28: 'God chose what is low and despised in the world, things that are not, to reduce to nothing things that are.'

Philippians 3.8: '. . . I regard everything as loss because of the surpassing value of knowing Christ Jesus my Lord. For his sake I have suffered the loss of all things, and I regard them as rubbish, in order that I may gain Christ.'

Allow the group to continue to reflect in silence. You may wish to draw this time to a close by re-reading Philippians 3.8, and inviting people to share what they've gained of Christ through this activity.

Note

You could use this idea for intercession – **Redeeming Rubbish** – by collecting rubbish solely from your neighbourhood, and adding into your display cards with negative words or quotes you've overheard on them, e.g.: 'I'm no good'; 'What's the point?'; Unemployment; Violence. Light a candle in the middle and pray for Christ's light to break into the lives of those who see themselves as rubbish.

Part 2

WEAVING PRAYER
THROUGH THE YEAR

6

Advent

———◦◆◦———

Advent is the beginning of the Christian year, and derives its meaning from the Latin for 'arrival'. In this season we anticipate Christ's coming, both in his long-promised incarnation, and in the fulfilment of his promise to return. The prayer themes of Advent centre on preparing to meet with Christ.

We worship in confident expectation of God's faithfulness in responding to his people's cry for deliverance. In our intercessions we express our longing, hope and expectation for Christ's Light to break into a dark and wayward world, exposing evil, bringing healing, and establishing the righteous rule of God's Kingdom. We wait with quiet confidence, identifying with those in the Scriptures who trusted God's promises of the coming Messiah. We make ourselves ready to meet our Lord as we journey through repentance to a renewed focus on Kingdom priorities.

There is also a contemplative aspect to Advent. As we wait, we make space for the Living Christ to be formed within, even as he silently grew within Mary. We too are called to be Christ-bearers.

In this reflective season, we turn aside from the world's ways by setting aside quiet time to prepare for the Saviour's birth, instead of rushing relentlessly after parties and presents.

(58) LIGHTS ON OUR WAY

Lighting a candle is an ancient church ritual. Candlelight can create an atmosphere. (No wonder it's a key ingredient to a romantic evening!) As we come to prayer, lighting a candle can help mark out sacred space and time, and create a sense of holiness, intimacy and silence. When harsh artificial light is turned down, candlelight provides a gentle, central focus that banishes outer distractions to the shadows.

A lit candle can symbolize Christ, the Light of the World, as we intercede for his light to come into dark places. It can express a personal prayer for Christ's light to shine through us. A candle can stand for the issue or person for whom we are praying. Lighting it is a prayer we can do and see.

As the candle burns on, it represents our continuous heart-cry to God, enabling us to 'pray at all times'. Candlelit vigils at times of grief are powerful as they hold our loss and loved ones before the Lord.

Candles can be used in prayer in many ways. Who will light them and when? Will they be lit from a central candle, or from one another as the light is passed round the group? Where will you place your candle: on a map, by a cross, or held in your hand?

The candle is a particularly appropriate symbol for the Advent hope of the coming of Christ's light to break into the darkness. Thus the first two prayer suggestions in this section involve lighting candles: one for thanksgiving, the other for intercession.

You will need one large white candle set up on a table next to a wall and enough tea-light candles placed around it for everyone in the group, plus some spare candles for those who wish to light more than one.

You will also need a mirror that you can stand behind the candles against the wall.

Explain how at Advent we anticipate the coming of Jesus, the Light of the World, yet there are those who have already made Jesus real to us through who they are and what they've said or done in our lives. In our prayer time we will remember these people.

Light the large candle and either turn out or dim other light sources in the room. Ask everyone to bring to mind someone who has shown them the light of Christ, and for whom they want to give thanks. When they are aware of someone in particular, people come to light a tea-light from the main candle, and place it on the table with a prayer such as: '**Lord, thank you for Joanne, who has shown the light of Jesus to me.**' Continue until all have had an opportunity to pray, which some may do more than once.

Now place the mirror behind the lit candles. Remind the group that the light they've seen in the lives of other Christians is a reflection of Jesus, the Light of the World. We too are called to reflect Christ's light to others. Allow some moments for a silent prayer response to this. Finish by reading Jesus' words in John 8.12: '**I am the light of the world. Whoever follows me will never walk in darkness but will have the light of life.**' Thanks be to God. Amen.

(59) LIGHT IN THE DARKNESS

You will need one large white candle and several tea-light candles set up on a low central table.

Light the central candle and turn out any artificial light in the room. Allow a few moments for the group to settle and focus their attention on the candle flame. Note how much impact the light, even of a single candle, can have on dark surroundings.

Read John 1.1–9.

As we approach Christmas and the coming of Christ, we ask the light of the world to shine afresh in dark places. Ask the group to remain quiet and allow God to bring to mind an area of darkness where they want to pray for the light of Christ to break in; it could be a place, a particular person or group of people, a wider social problem or even a world situation.

After some moments, encourage the group to pray for Christ's light to shine by lighting a tea-light from the central candle. They can do this in silence, or accompany their action with brief words such as, '**Lord Jesus, may your light shine into Sarah's life**', or '**Lord Jesus, may your light dispel the darkness of drug-dealing in our town**', etc. Have enough candles for people to offer more than one prayer if they wish.

Finally, reflect on how the light has increased as more candles have been lit from the source of the central 'Christ-candle'. You may wish to conclude by re-reading John 1.5: '**The light shines in the darkness, and the darkness did not overcome it.**'

(60) LET GO, LET BE, LET JESUS

Prayer is not only talking to God, but also a time to let go our concerns in total trust and simply enjoy being in his presence.

Total silence can be a challenge in our noisy world. If group members find themselves frustrated by restless thoughts in this exercise, remind them God hears and honours their heart's intent, even if their mind's content has proved troublingly overactive on this occasion.

The appropriate length of time will vary according to how used people are to shared quietness. Five minutes may well be long enough for an inexperienced group to taste the silence.

You will not need anything at all, unless you feel your group would find some gentle background music more helpful than complete silence.

Explain that as we prepare for Christ's coming in Advent, we particularly focus on making room to receive God, just as Mary made space for Jesus to grow quietly inside her body. So we are not going to fill this prayer time with words and requests, but simply let go in quiet acceptance and be still in God's presence, allowing him to come into our lives and do as he wills.

The prayer leader guides and holds the silence

Settle yourself into a posture so that you are comfortable, but alert . . . Be aware of your breathing . . . and allow it to become slower . . . calmer . . . deeper . . . Let go. Let be. Let Jesus . . . Allow yourself to become aware of any tension in your body . . . and relax that part . . . breathing out and letting the tension go . . . Let go. Let be. Let Jesus . . . Allow these words, 'Let go. Let be. Let Jesus' to resonate round your being . . . breathe them in and let them settle quietly inside. . . . Rest in the Lord's presence in silent attentiveness, and if any distracting thoughts emerge, allow the words 'Let go. Let be. Let Jesus' to come to mind and gently draw you back to inner quietness . . . (*Extended time of silence*) . . .

Let go. Let be. Let Jesus . . . Take your own time to come out of the silence and open your eyes to this room around you, knowing that you still remain in the Lord's presence.

Invite the group to share their experience of the silence together. Could they learn to pause in the middle of busy, everyday activities and take a few moments just to 'Let go. Let be. Let Jesus'?

(61) JOURNEYING WITH JESUS

The Christian life is a journey with Jesus. Although this idea is linked to Advent, it could be adapted with a suitable introduction to other journeys: Abraham's journey of faith, Jesus' call or commissioning of the disciples, Paul's missionary journeys, etc. You may wish to choose a selection of the objects rather than include them all.

You will need a small suitcase and appropriate objects as a focus for the prayers, e.g. a heavy stone, two clocks, a child's toy, an apron, family photograph, apple, empty box and gift-wrapped item.

Explain that as the season of preparing for Christ's birth, Advent is the beginning of the Christian church year – the start of a journey. God continually calls us to make journeys with him. This means letting go of our past, responding to his call in the present, and leaving our 'comfort zones' for the unknown of the glorious future God has planned for us.

Place the open suitcase centrally and put in it the stone, two clocks and the toy. Distribute the other objects among the group (it will help you to know who has got what!), and explain that the prayers will involve people as you ask them to remove or pack particular objects as appropriate.

The prayer leader guides the prayers

In this prayer time, we are focusing on our call to follow Jesus, and imagine we are packing our life's suitcase ready for the journey ahead.

As we respond to Jesus' call we pray:

Leader: Lord of the journey,
All: **Hear our prayer and lead us on.**

Sometimes we continue to carry heavy burdens that we need to lay down.
(*Ask for the stone to be taken out of the case*)
What do you need to take out of your case that you've dragged around for too long?
(*Pause*)

Leader: Lord of the journey,
All: **Hear our prayer and lead us on.**

Sometimes we fill our case with unnecessary items, things we won't have time for.
(*Ask for one of the clocks to be taken out of the case*)
Is your case overpacked with too much to do? What do you need to leave behind?
(*Pause*)

Leader: Lord of the journey,
All: **Hear our prayer and lead us on.**

Sometimes we pack our bag with things we have outgrown, and don't need any more.
(*Ask for the toy to be taken out of the case*)
Is there something in your life that has outlived its usefulness? What do you need to leave behind?
(*Pause*)

Leader: Lord of the journey,
All: **Hear our prayer and lead us on.**

When we go away, we pack the clothing we need for what we are going to be doing.
(*Ask for the apron to be placed in the case*)
What resources of Christ and his character do you need to be clothed in as you go on your way?
(*Pause*)

Leader: Lord of the journey,
All: **Hear our prayer and lead us on.**

Sometimes we take things that are precious to us – personal mementoes.
(*Ask for the photograph to be placed in the case*)
What thanksgivings and blessings do you want to take with you to cherish?
(*Pause*)

Leader: Lord of the journey,
All: **Hear our prayer and lead us on.**

Sometimes we take food to sustain us as we travel.
(*Ask for the apple to be placed in the case*)
What do we want to feed on as we journey? Is there a word of Scripture, a blessing or encouragement that particularly sustains us?
(*Pause*)

Leader: Lord of the journey,
All: **Hear our prayer and lead us on.**

We also need to leave space in our case for things we will acquire on the way.
(*Ask for the open box to be placed in the case*)
What blessings do you hope for in your journey? Pray for them.
(*Pause*)

Leader: Lord of the journey,
All: **Hear our prayer and lead us on.**

Often we take gifts for others we will meet on our journey.
(*Ask for the gift-wrapped item to be placed in the case*)
What will you take to give away?
(*Pause*)

Leader: Lord of the journey,
All: **Hear our prayer and lead us on,**
Leader: Along the paths of your purposes into the place you have prepared for us in your eternal kingdom. In Jesus' name.
All: **Amen.**

(62) ROUND TUIT

How often do people say they'll finish that job when they get around to it? By receiving a 'Round Tuit' in the form of a circular plate, they now have what they need to complete the task! Advent can be seen as God's Round Tuit, a season that prompts action and helps us prioritize as we anticipate Jesus' imminent return.

You will need some felt-tip pens and small paper plates, one of which you have used to make a sample Round Tuit, by decorating the edge and writing 'Round Tuit' in the centre. Background music – perhaps an Advent hymn – would be helpful for the concluding reflection.

Explain that often we put off necessary jobs because we haven't got around to it. Show them the sample Round Tuit: once you have one of these, there's no excuse for not clearing out the loft, etc.

During Advent we not only prepare to celebrate Christ's birth, but anticipate his return, in the Second Coming that will mark the end of the age and the start of the new creation. What would we be doing differently now if we knew Christ was coming back *this* Christmas?

Invite everyone to take a paper plate to make an Advent Round Tuit. In the centre, they write the Lord's promise from Revelation 22.20: **'Surely I am coming soon'**, adding colourful decoration around it so the plate attracts the attention.

As they do this, ask people to chat in pairs around how they'd feel about Christ coming back soon. How would priorities change? Are there things they know they'd now make time to do?

Once everyone has finished, ask each person to swap Round Tuits with his or her partner.

Ask people to place the Round Tuit they've received on their lap and focus on the central words, in an attitude of openness. As you put on the background music, invite people quietly to tune into God, asking him how he would have them respond *now* to prepare for Christ's coming. Allow some time for this.

As you close this exercise, encourage people to take their Advent Round Tuit home, perhaps placing it next to their Advent calendar. As it catches their eye, it will underline the priorities the Spirit has prompted them with in this prayer time. The challenge is then to respond!

7

Christmas

As Advent draws to a close the season of waiting becomes a festival of welcome and celebration of the birth of Emmanuel, God with us. The prayer themes of Christmas centre on joyful praise and wonder at the God who has sent his Son among us.

In humility we worship him who is King of all, yet willing to be born in a stable. We join with the angels to praise and proclaim the Prince of Peace, and we pray for others to recognize the true identity of the baby in the manger as the Saviour of the world. We respond personally to the Lord as in imagination we accompany the shepherds and kings to the stable, and bow before the newborn Christ to offer the gift of our worship and our very selves.

The world around us may seek to reduce Christmas to merely a sentimental and nostalgic festival 'for the children', but we know differently. While we respond with child-like trust and spontaneous joy to the Christ-child, we never forget that the one who lies in the Crib will suffer the Cross before wearing the Crown of Glory.

(63) PASS THE PARCEL

So many outer distractions can hide the real meaning of Christmas. This exercise links this theme to a Christmas party game. Fading the music down gradually each time will ensure

no one is put on the spot, but enable people to volunteer a
prayer response.

---

*You will need a small box and a symbol of the Christ-child to put
inside. This could be the crib and/or baby from a Nativity set, or
simply a piece of coloured card with the word 'Emmanuel' written
on it. The box should then be wrapped in several layers of Christmas
wrapping paper, as for a game of Pass the Parcel.*

*You will also need some music to play, preferably something with
a Christmas flavour.*

Have the group sit in a circle and pass the parcel around as the
music is played. Fade the music down from time to time, and
ask people to think of some aspect of the Christmas season
that blocks our view of Jesus (e.g. overeating and drinking,
consumerism and pressure to spend, stress and strain in fam-
ilies, loneliness). Invite anyone to keep hold of the parcel, speak
out a 'block', and unwrap the next layer of paper as a prayer
for this barrier to be removed. While the unwrapping is a
prayer in itself, it could be accompanied by simple words such
as, **'Lord, please take away this layer, and help us see you
more clearly this Christmas.'** Others may wish to add their
own prayers.

As the final wrapping is removed and the Christ-child re-
vealed, ask people to think of whom they would like to pass
Jesus on to this Christmas, and say their names out loud or
offer them in silence. Encourage some prayers of praise and
thanksgiving for Emmanuel – God with us. You may prefer to
finish with a Christmas carol!

(64) CHRISTMAS CRACKER PRAYERS

This exercise combines the fun of a hands-on activity with that of coming up with creative ideas for prayer topics together. As such it can appeal to groups of all ages, and hopefully the exercise won't be forgotten among the fun of pulling crackers at other times during Christmas celebrations.

You will need a box of Christmas crackers, of sufficient quality to contain novelty gifts alongside paper hats.

Give each person a cracker and invite group members in turn to pull their cracker with a partner. As each one is pulled revealing the gift inside, ask people to link this object to an appropriate prayer – an intercession or perhaps a thanksgiving. Group members then offer this prayer, or prayers, and the next cracker is pulled.

(Examples of gifts and prayers might be:

A ring: a prompt to pray for those we love
A puzzle: a prompt to pray for the healing of those whose lives are in pieces
A mini tool-kit: a prompt to pray for those who have to work over Christmas
A toy car: a prompt to pray for safety on the roads. And so on.)

Ask people to put on the party hats enclosed in their crackers, and finish the prayer time by thanking God for the coming of Jesus and all he has done for us. Once we were 'not a people', but now we have become '. . . **a chosen race, a royal priesthood, a holy nation, God's own people**' (1 Peter 2.9).

(65) NATIVITY PRAYERS

You will need Nativity-set figures. Some gentle, background Christmas music will enhance this prayer activity.

Distribute the different figures among the group members, and place the infant Jesus in the manger centrally as the foremost element of the Nativity scene.

Explain that our prayers will be linked to the various figures in the Nativity story.

Start by asking the group to focus on the infant Jesus – Emmanuel, God with us, in all his vulnerability. After some space for reflection, invite those who wish to offer prayers of praise and thanksgiving to God, for sending us his Son.

The infant figure can prompt us to think of our young ones. Invite people to pray for our children over this Christmas season.

Next, ask whoever has Mary to place her into the scene and to suggest a connection to people and Christmas prayer needs that she might represent. Allow some moments for quiet reflection on the expanded scene, and then invite short, spoken prayers around the link along the lines suggested.

Continue in this way, with Joseph, shepherds and sheep, kings and gifts being placed around the crib, one after another. The prayer links can be quite simple, e.g.:

Mary:	mothers, those far from home, the call to trust and obedience
Joseph:	fathers, family unity at Christmas-time
Shepherds:	those working at Christmas; those needing to hear the good news of Jesus

112

Sheep/Animals:	our care for creation; pets bought as Christmas presents
Kings:	those with power and status in society, for humility and wisdom
The gifts:	ourselves, and how we might give to Jesus this Christmas

Conclude by asking everyone to focus again on Jesus at the centre of the scene, and pray that he might indeed be at the heart of our Christmas.

Finish, if appropriate, with a Christmas song or carol, or by sharing the Peace together.

(66) FILL THE SKIES WITH PRAISE

You will need a large piece of black paper or cloth with which to cover a table with a dark background, plus some pens.

You will also need to prepare a number of white paper-angel shapes, and a copy of Luke 2.14 for all to see.

Background music that sets an exuberant, celebratory tone of worship could help lift this prayer activity into the heavenlies! The 'Hallelujah Chorus' from Handel's Messiah *would be a good choice.*

Read the story of the angels appearing before the shepherds to announce Christ's birth in Luke 2.8–14. The dazzling announcement of Emmanuel, God with us, broke into the darkness before the shepherds' eyes. The skies were ablaze with praise as the host of angels proclaimed the glory of God and celebrated his coming among humankind.

Explain that we are going to create our own praising host by writing personal prayers of praise and thanksgiving on the paper angels, and placing them on our own dark 'sky'

113

background. These prayers might include thanksgivings for things God has done in our lives over the last year.

Allow some time for this, and have enough angels available for people to write more than one prayer, to create a respectably numerous celestial throng.

Finish by joyfully declaring the angels' praise in Luke 2.14 together: **'Glory to God in the highest heaven, and on earth peace among those whom he favours!'** Amen.

(67) PARENTING THE CHRIST-CHILD

At Christmas we often feel caught up in activity, busy with hospitality and socializing, and with very little space for ourselves. Having prayer stations where people have the freedom and space to respond and reflect at their own pace can be especially valuable over this season.

It can take time and effort to set up prayer stations beforehand, but it's well worth it. During the activity itself, the leader's challenge is to step back and simply allow people to explore and pray as they feel led, trusting God to do the rest.

You could position the four prayer stations in the corners of a large room, or even use different rooms if this is appropriate to your meeting place. Otherwise you could section one large main table, or limit your stations to a couple of the suggestions below if space is tight.

You will need some gentle background music for this exercise, plus the elements for four separate prayer stations. Each station should have some visual representation of the Holy Family, such as a Christmas card, Nativity-set figures or painting, and a lit candle for Christ, the Light of the World. In addition each station will have visual aids or symbols connected with the particular parenting theme, and copies of a Bible reference plus questions for reflection.

Some visual aids are suggested below. You may think of others. If you cannot provide them yourself and can't find a friendly young parent to help you out, you could cut out relevant pictures from a parenting magazine and stick them up on card for a simple display.

The four prayer stations are as follows:

Station (1) Welcoming the Christ-child

Symbols: New Baby greeting cards, baby sling, baby monitor, washing powder, stain remover, coins, clock.

Bible verses: Luke 2.8–20.

Reflection: Reflect on the impact a baby's birth has on new parents. Life is never the same again. It takes a whole new direction and dimension, affecting relationships, time, money – and sleep! What changes has the life of Jesus born in you brought into your life?

Station (2) Nurturing the Christ-child

Symbols: Baby's bottle, baby food, blanket, dummy, baby lotion, nappy.

Bible verses: Luke 2.1–7.

Reflection: Reflect on the work involved in looking after a small baby: the day-to-day routines of feeding, clothing, bathing, dressing, protecting and caring for the child. What equivalent activities do you undertake as you nurture the life of Jesus within you?

Station (3) Growing the Christ-child

Symbols: Birth or baptism certificates, baptism cards or gifts, doctor's appointment cards, playgroup fliers, toys, pram suit, mittens.

Bible verses: Luke 2.21, 27–40.

Reflection: Reflect on the ways in which a baby gains an identity and place out in the world, through baptism or dedication, a name on official documentation, joining a playgroup, etc. In what ways does Christ's life in you become recognized by those around you? How do people know he lives within you?

Station (4) Releasing the Christ-child

Symbols: Photos of a young schoolchild, children's book, plasters, children's shoes.

Bible verses: Luke 2.41–51.

Reflection: Reflect on how the task of parenting develops as the baby becomes the child who starts school and begins to move towards independence and the responsibilities of adulthood. What does it feel like to parent a child through these stages? How might God be calling you to release the Christ-life within into a fuller maturity, perhaps taking you beyond your comfort zone and on to new horizons?

Explain that the prayer stations are set up for people to use as they choose, and agree the time available for this activity (perhaps around fifteen minutes). People may spend time at all, some or one of the stations, as they prefer.

Play some quiet music and allow people to wander round, sit and pray. At the end of the allotted time, ask them to return. Allow the music to continue and invite people, if they wish, to share something of their reflections. Ensure people know these contributions are not for discussion or debate. The group will simply listen and receive the insights offered without intrusive comment.

You may wish to finish this time by saying the Grace together.

8

Lent and Holy Week

———◆◆———

The word Lent derives from the Anglo-Saxon for 'lengthen', referring to the lengthening of days during spring. This forty-day period of preparation preceding Easter is linked with the period of Jesus' temptation in the wilderness, and thus has become a season of spiritual spring-cleaning and inner renewal. The prayer themes of Lent centre on following Jesus in total commitment, to be prepared and matured for ministry.

As we look to Jesus in the wilderness, we praise the one who remained wholly obedient through all temptations. We thank him for understanding and forgiving our frailty. In our intercessions we remember those who struggle to survive in the barrenness of the world's deserts, physical and spiritual. We pray for Christians who endure particular hardships for the sake of the gospel. We may respond to God's prompting by undertaking a personal spiritual journey through the desert, abstaining from particular physical comforts that we might be spiritually purified. We face our hungers, temptations and destructive passions and allow the Lord to minister to us in those hard places. We let go of things we have and do to discover afresh who we are in Christ.

While the world may follow Christmas indulgence with diets and disciplines to improve self-image and enhance physical health, we adopt such practices to allow the image of Christ to be formed within us and open ourselves up to a deeper spiritual wholeness.

(68) ASH WEDNESDAY ANOINTING

The practice of abstaining from something for Lent harbours the danger of taking undue pride in our self-discipline. Marking the start of this period with an anointing of ashes, composed of our own burnt offerings mingled with those of a burnt cross, can help us focus on obedience to Christ rather than our own achievements.

You will need enough small crosses for everyone. Traditionally this practice uses palm crosses from the previous year. However, you could make an equivalent batch from light, dry twigs or pampas grass, tied with cotton. You will also need slips of paper and pens for each person.

To prepare the ash you will need matches, a metal waste bin (and a bucket of sand in case of emergency!) set up outside. You will also need a small bowl and some olive oil. The latter is mixed with the ash to form a paste for the anointing part of the exercise.

Explain that we're going to draw on the ancient church tradition of 'the imposition of ashes' on Ash Wednesday as we start the season of Lent. As Lent is a time for penitence, we may be aware of things we want to let go of in our Christian lives: a habit, a besetting sin, an unhealthy dependency on something other than Christ. As it is a time of purification, we may be intending to abstain from some habit or comfort, to deepen our discipleship. In this prayer activity we will bring these things before God, so we can turn from our past and focus on following Christ through our personal disciplines.

Pass round the slips of paper and crosses and invite each person to write down whatever they want Christ to put to death in them during Lent.

The group now takes these outside. Set light to your paper and cross in the metal bin and invite people to drop their crosses and paper into the flame in turn. When everything has been burnt and the bin begun to cool, take out some of the ash and put it in a small bowl. Add in a small amount of olive oil to mix it into a paste.

Now invite the group to anoint one another with ash and oil. The bowl is passed round the group. Each one dips a finger in it and then traces the sign of the cross on the wrist, hand or forehead of the next person, as appropriate. The one anointing his or her neighbour offers a prayer, such as: '**Jane, may Christ put to death all in you that is not of him, and enable you to follow him in Spirit and in truth.**'

Note

You could simplify this activity by preparing the ash beforehand, though this will mean losing some of the symbolic significance inherent in the full exercise.

(69) OFFERING OUR WHOLE SELVES TO GOD

The key to corporate prayer is participation. Using this meditative focus on our bodies encourages an active involvement in prayer in a different way from praying out loud. It may need to be led with sensitivity or adapted for a group which includes those struggling with physical pain or disability.

Ask the group to remain seated but to close their eyes.

The prayer leader guides the meditation

In Romans, Paul urges that we offer our bodies as living sacrifices, holy and pleasing to God, for this is our spiritual act of worship.

Assume a posture of relaxed alertness . . . Be still . . . Calm and deepen your breathing . . . Breathe in the Lord's presence and sustenance . . . Sense his Spirit flowing into and through you as his child, abiding in him . . . God is holding your body in being.

Become aware of your *head* – eyes, ears, nose, mouth – mind. Think about what goes on as you process information through your senses. Our head is the place of knowing, learning, deciding, controlling our body and our purposes. We are called to be transformed by the renewal of our minds. Where does your mind need transforming? In quietness offer your thinking and decision-making to the Lord. (*Pause*)

Moving down our bodies, we come to our *shoulders*. This area can be one of tension as we carry burdens and anxieties. Tense up your shoulders and then let them relax as a silent prayer of letting go, and casting your cares upon the Lord.

Now we move our focus on to our *arms*, becoming aware of how they feel . . . the sensation of sleeve on skin . . . right down to our hands and fingers . . . Wiggle your fingers, tense them and relax as a reminder of how they can move . . . With our hands we work and serve others. What daily tasks occupy your hands? Offer your hands to the Lord for his service. (*Pause*)

A hand can stretch out in friendship or form a fist of hostility. Where do you need to extend a hand of peace instead of pushing away? Offer your hands to the Lord for reconciliation and healing. (*Pause*)

Now we bring our attention down into the *central part of our body*. Here are organs vital to life. Here the heart continuously pumps our blood . . . Become aware of your heartbeat. Thank the Lord for the gift of your life, and offer it back to him.

We move down to the *stomach and gut*, organs concerned with taking in nourishment and nurture, and organs concerned with reproduction and fruitfulness. We welcome the Spirit into these intimate places of our being . . . And as he fills them, we sense him touch on things we feel too deeply even for words . . . So we allow the Spirit to stir up within us those personal situations where we've run out of things to say because they're too distressing, full of so much yearning, or too overwhelming, or too unjust, or have been going on too long . . . And we offer them up to the Lord with a sigh, a heart-cry beyond words.

We move on down through the body to the *legs*, these limbs that bring the gift of mobility . . . Become aware of these muscles of movement right down through thighs, calves and feet to your toes . . . Wiggle your toes, tense them and relax . . . Scripture says how lovely on the mountains are the feet of those who bring good news. Our mobility is a gift to be cherished and used wisely. Offer your journeys, your comings and goings to the Lord, that you may always be a bringer of good news.

Become aware now again of your entire body as you sit . . . the rising and falling of your breathing . . . your whole being, created . . . and sustained . . . and loved . . . and held by God . . . And committed to his service.

Lord, we offer our bodies as living sacrifices, holy and pleasing to God, for this is our spiritual act of worship. Amen.

(70) WHO AM I IN THE DESERT?

You will need a tall, white candle and a cross to represent Christ, and a set of objects symbolizing things in life that we have, do and achieve. These could include money, house keys, passport, diary, driving licence, an ID card from a workplace, an item of jewellery, exam certificate, a TV remote control, and so on. Use your creative imagination to compile whatever objects will be meaningful to your particular group. You will also need to distribute copies of the prayer responses.

Place the candle and all the other objects except the cross on a central table (or even a tray of sand!), with the candle in the middle.

Explain that as Christ went into the wilderness, vulnerable and alone, yet grounded in the knowledge of his identity as God's Son, so during Lent we remind ourselves of who we are in Christ, even when our outer 'layers' of possessions, achievements and activities are stripped away.

Start the prayer time by lighting the candle that symbolizes Christ, the Light of Life. Invite each person in turn to take an object off the table and put it underneath or to one side, using the following format.

Person praying: (*Removes the chosen object*)

Who am I when _____ is taken away from my life?
(*Pause for reflection. What would it feel like to be without that particular 'layer'?*)

Leader: The Lord says, 'Fear not, for I have redeemed you. I have called you by name; you are mine.'
All: **My life is hidden with Christ in God, and none can snatch me from his hand.**

Continue round the group until all the objects have been removed. Allow some final moments for reflection on the 'Christ-candle', the Light of Life that remains amidst the emptiness.

Conclude by placing the cross next to the candle and reading Philippians 2.5–8.

(71) CENTRED ON JESUS

You will simply need enough room for all to stand with sufficient space around them.

You may wish to use some quiet music for this activity; an instrumental version of 'Jesus be the centre' would be especially suitable.

Explain at Lent we focus particularly on the Christian discipline of keeping our whole selves centred on Jesus. For this prayer-meditation we will stand in his presence, and offer to him aspects of our lives where we're tempted to go 'off-centre'.

Ask people to stand so they have enough space around them to move a step in any direction without bumping into their neighbour. They may wish to take off their shoes before moving into position to indicate that they stand on the holy ground of Christ's presence as they pray.

The prayer leader guides the prayers

As you stand, become aware of your body . . . If it helps, close your eyes . . . Keep your weight evenly on both feet . . . Hunch up your shoulders and let them relax . . . Allow your arms to drop down naturally at your side . . . Release any tension in your body . . . Relax, but stand tall and straight, without slouching . . . You are in the presence of the King of Kings . . .

Imagine that you stand in a shaft of bright light, like a spotlight . . . the light of Jesus, the Light of the World . . . Bask in the light of his loving presence shining down . . . enfolding you . . . protecting you . . . loving you . . . Respond and receive all the life and light he's pouring upon you . . . In the centre of his loving will you are held in his perfect place, but sometimes you're tempted to stray out of Jesus' light . . .

As you stand, bring to mind the times when you want to run ahead of his light . . . when you're impatient for him to act . . . where you're tempted to rush when Jesus bids you wait or walk . . . As these things come to mind, take a step forward, out of the light . . . and in the quiet, give these areas over to Jesus . . . Use some silent gesture of offering, or placing these things into Jesus' care . . . Let them go . . . and as an act of trust in his perfect timing, step back again into his light . . . Bask in Jesus' light as you stay in his presence . . .

Now become aware of the distractions that come alongside you as you follow Jesus . . . Where do you get sidetracked from serving him? . . . What takes your attention away from loving him with all you have and are? . . . As these distractions come to mind, step to your right, out of the light . . . and offer a silent gesture of laying these things down before Jesus, that they might not draw you aside from your walk with him . . . Let them go . . . and to convey your intention to stay centred on Jesus, step back to the left again, into his light of his presence . . . Bask in his light as you focus fully on him alone . . .

Now bring to mind the difficulties and obstacles you meet as you follow Jesus . . . the ones that seem too hard to overcome . . . where you just want to give up and walk away . . . As these things come to mind, step over to your left, out of the light . . . Use a silent gesture to place your difficulties at Jesus' feet . . . and express your openness to let him work as he wills, even through these situations . . . and now, step back right, into the centre again, to convey your desire to stay faithful to Christ, even when the way is rough . . . Bask in his light . . . allow him to strengthen you with his power to persevere . . .

Now become aware of the places where you are reluctant to follow . . . the things that cause you to hesitate and fear . . . As these come to mind, take a step backwards, out of the light, for where you lag behind the light of Jesus and hang back from where he would lead you . . . Use some gesture to offer these fears, doubts and misgivings to Jesus, that he might dispel them . . . And now step forward again into the light, the centre of Jesus' presence, to convey your willingness to move forward in him, focused on his strength, not your own fears . . . Bask in the loving light of Jesus' presence . . . Allow him to hold you . . . to strengthen you . . . to love you . . . and sense his joy as you respond to him . . .

When you're ready, open your eyes, and come back into this room, but remember that as you have centred on him, he remains within, and 'the one who is in you is greater than the one who is in the world'.* **Thanks be to God. Amen.**

(72) END TO HOSTILITIES

This idea will work best during Holy Week, as you will need a palm cross for each person, and a small, central standing cross in the middle of the group.

Some background music, such as a Passiontide hymn or song, or a classical 'Agnus Dei', would enhance this exercise, which should not be rushed.

Give each person a palm cross and ask them to grasp it in their hands with the long side away from them, as if they were holding a sword.

* 1 John 4.4

Explain that through his death on the cross, Christ has overcome the power of the sword with the power of God's reconciling love.

Open the prayer time by reading Colossians 1.19–20: '**For in [Christ] all the fullness of God was pleased to dwell, and through him God was pleased to reconcile to himself all things, whether on earth or in heaven, by making peace through the blood of his cross.**' Ask people to let the Spirit bring to mind a place or situation in the world where hostilities need to cease and the peace of Christ be allowed to rule. As these occur, invite people in their own time to turn round the 'sword' in their hand so they now hold a cross, and place this on the table around the central cross, with a simple prayer to be affirmed by a response together:

Person praying: Jesus, by the blood of your Cross bring peace to . . .
All: **Amen. Come, Lord Jesus.**

When all have turned their swords to crosses, allow some space for quiet reflection. Close the prayer time with further words from Colossians (3.15): '**Let the peace of Christ rule in your hearts to which indeed you were called in the one body.**' Invite the group to share Christ's Peace with one another, in response to his call.

(73) BROKEN FOR ME, BROKEN FOR YOU

You will need some longish dry sticks or twigs. One of these should be 'planted' in earth in a pot, to stand in the middle of the group, with the other sticks on the table in front.

'When I survey the wondrous Cross' would be particularly appropriate as background music.

Open the prayer time by asking the group to focus their attention on the planted stick as you read Isaiah 53.1–3, and to reflect on Jesus, the Suffering Servant.

Then ask people to pick up one of the sticks on the table. As you introduce each section, invite people to make their own silent prayers as they bring each 'stick' to Christ in the pauses before the shared response.

Leader: Here is the stick we see wielded in wars across the earth. (*Pause*)
Lord, have mercy.
All: **Christ, have mercy.**

Leader: Here is the stick we fear as others come against us. (*Pause*)
Lord, have mercy.
All: **Christ, have mercy.**

Leader: Here is the stick we raise in anger against others. (*Pause*)
Lord, have mercy.
All: **Christ, have mercy.**

Leader: Here is the stick with which we beat ourselves. (*Pause*)
Lord, have mercy.
All: **Christ, have mercy.**

Read on in Isaiah 53.4–6, and then ask people to break their sticks and place them on the table in the shape of a cross. End with an open time of thanksgiving for all Christ has done for us.

As those whose hands no longer hold sticks and so can be open in love to one another, finish by joining hands to say the Grace together.

9

Easter

We've come through the turbulent emotions of Holy Week: the excitement of Palm Sunday; the poignancy of the Last Supper; the agony of Good Friday and the numb grief of Holy Saturday. Finally, on Easter Sunday, joy breaks forth. Christ is risen! Alleluia! Easter stands as the greatest festival of the Christian year. Its prayer themes centre on a resounding affirmation of the Lord who has conquered the grave.

Praises and thanksgivings overflow as we celebrate Jesus' victory over sin and death. The season of fasting gives way to one of feasting on the abundant life that pours forth from the empty tomb. We intercede with faith that nothing is impossible for God, and pray for new life to come into dead situations, for implacable opposites to be reconciled, for what seem like endings to become beginnings through God's mighty transforming power. In our personal prayers we gain courage to leave the past behind, taste the joy of Jesus in the present, and look with confidence to let him lead us forward in new directions.

As those around us merely look forward to a long weekend of lying-in or dabbling in DIY, we find ourselves caught up in celebrating life in all its fullness, and the renewal of the cosmos through the triumph of Christ.

(74) RECONCILING OPPOSITES

You will need different-coloured pieces of card on which you have written paired opposites: e.g. Black/White, Management/Workforce, Male/Female and so on (one word per card). Use current events and issues in the local community and church to suggest other opposing factions, and leave some cards blank among your set.

You will also need some felt-tip pens and a small, standing cross.

Place the cards face up at one end of a central table and the cross at the other end. The cards should be shuffled so the pairings are not next to one another.

Explain that Jesus died and rose again to open up the way of reconciliation both between God and the human race, and between each other.

Invite people to find a matching pair of opposites and place them together near the cross, along with a short prayer that these groups be reconciled with one another and be brought closer to Christ. Others can add their prayers out loud or in silence.

When the written cards have been used up, ask people to allow other 'opposites' they wish to be reconciled to come to mind. Invite them to write these pairings on different cards and place them together by the cross, along with a prayer for reconciliation.

As God's family, reconciled to one another, unite by finishing this prayer time in saying the Grace together.

(75) JESUS DIED FOR THESE . . .

You will need a large standing cross (a home-made one in a pot of earth could be very effective), some Post-it notes and pens.

Place the cross centrally and have Post-its and pens available.

Read out John 3.16: **'For God so loved the world that he gave his only Son, that everyone who believes in him may not perish but have eternal life.'**

Ask people to write on a Post-it note the name of someone they want to see come to Christ. Invite them to stick the note somewhere on the cross as their prayer. You could invite them to say, as they do so, **'Thank you, Lord, that you died for x.'**

Read Matthew 28.19–20: **'Go therefore and make disciples of all nations, baptizing them in the name of the Father and of the Son and of the Holy Spirit, and teaching them to obey everything that I have commanded you.'**

Ask people to be open to what the Lord might be calling them to do to bring the person into the Kingdom, and allow some moments for quiet reflection.

(76) CHANGED TIMES

This prayer activity takes the form of introductory sections read by the prayer leader, followed by an active response from the group at the end of each part.

You will need a loaf of bread, a key, and pumpkin or sunflower seeds in a small bowl.

Leader: There was a time when the dead stayed lifeless,
           when the end of the road was the end of the road.
           But Jesus is risen from the dead:
           he walked out of his tomb to meet Mary grieving in
           the garden.

So now nothing is lost and gone that cannot rise into something new.

Even the rubbish heap can yield grains of gold.

'So if anyone is in Christ, there is a new creation; everything old has passed away; see, everything has become new!'*

(The bowl of seeds is passed round the group. As each person holds it, he or she prays for new life and hope to come into a dead situation, either experienced or known about. The prayer can be made silently or out loud, **'Lord, please bring new life and hope into . . . '**.)

Leader: There was a time when a closed door stayed shut, when we locked ourselves away from what we could not face.

But Jesus is risen from the dead:

he came through locked doors to greet his fearful followers.

So now we can walk free of fear to face new challenges and opportunities,

even into the places where we've only dreamed of going.

'So if the Son makes you free, you will be free indeed.'**

(The key is passed round the group. Each person, holding it, prays for the ability to open the door to something he or she has previously hung back from. The prayer can be made silently or aloud, **'Lord, please help me open the door to . . . '**.)

* 2 Corinthians 5.17
** John 8.36

Leader: There was a time when we were left alone,
when we called out in our emptiness without being
sure anyone heard us.
But Jesus is risen from the dead:
he came to Galilee to break bread and eat with his
dear disciples.
So now we know his presence with us amidst human
frailty and faithlessness,
even through the darkest night.
'Remember I am with you always, to the end of the
age.'*

(The bread is passed round the group. Each person tears off a
piece and gives it to the next person to eat, saying the prayer,
'May you know Jesus is always with you.' The recipient, after
eating, takes the bread and gives a piece to his or her neighbour, and so on.)

Leader: Risen Lord,
may we sow the new life you offer.
May we go in faith through new doors.
May we know you with us always.
Amen.

(77) ALL THINGS MADE NEW

*You will need two contrasting sets of objects. For example, on
one tray place a piece of broken pottery, some withered flowers,
scribbled-on and screwed-up bits of paper, an empty water bottle,
and a dirty stone. On another tray place a whole cup, a thriving
potted plant, some fresh, clean sheets of paper, a full jug of water
and a precious stone or decorative glass nugget.*

* Matthew 28.20

Place these trays next to one another centrally, and between them put a piece of paper with EASTER DAY written on it.

Read the words of Jesus, enthroned as King in Revelation 21.5, where he declares: 'See, I am making all things new.' Explain that Jesus' resurrection victory has opened the way to life beyond death, and promised the renewal and regeneration of all creation.

Ask people to reflect on the transforming power of the resurrection and the wonder of all things made new, as they look at the objects in front of them, perhaps touching or handling them if they wish.

After an appropriate time of quiet, invite the group to pray short prayers of praise and thanksgiving, based on the insights and inspiration that have come to them through what they've seen and touched – just as the disciples saw and touched the resurrected body of Jesus himself.

Note

While the above idea is linked to praise and thanksgiving, it could be used to prompt prayers for healing and **Being made new,** by asking people to reflect on which object they identify with on one tray and/or wish to become on the second tray. They could then share their response in pairs or threes and pray for each other.

(78) EASTER GLORY

You may wish to adapt this basic idea by using music and words appropriate for your group, but the aim of this exercise is to celebrate God the Lord of all creation whose mighty power has raised Jesus from the dead.

While there are many collections of reflective music (see *Further resources*), compilations of uplifting music are harder to come by – a telling comment on our stressed culture, perhaps. An alternative music choice for this exercise could be 'See what a morning', sung by Margaret Becker, Joanne Hogg and Kristyn Lennox on the CD New Irish Hymns #2 (Kingsway Music 2003).

To set a celebratory tone you might also wish to consider Beethoven's 'Ode to Joy' from his 9th Symphony, Carl Orff's 'Ecce Gratum' from Carmina Burana, or the joyful Celtic 'Caracena' by Bill Whelan, the composer of Riverdance, on the CD 'Celtic Heartbeat Collection' *(Celtic Heartbeat 1995)*.

You will need words, music and a central visual focus. For words use either poems such as the exuberant 'Spring' or 'Pied Beauty' by Gerard Manley Hopkins, or liturgical praise such as the Gloria or Te Deum *from the Anglican* Common Worship *book.*

Use Vivaldi's 'Gloria' as an uplifting accompaniment.

For your display place a green cloth over the table and lay a mirror over it to form a base for the centrepiece: a vase of bright, spring flowers – such as daffodils – encircled with candles. The mirror will catch and reflect the candlelight.

Explain that we are going to allow the Spirit to lift our hearts in praise to our glorious and victorious God in Christ through words, music and visual display.

Light the candles and start the music. Let the musical introduction play and begin to read the poem/Gloria aloud as the first words are sung. Read without rushing and allow the music to continue to its end after you have finished, so everyone can continue in quiet rejoicing as they listen.

At the end of the piece, you may wish to encourage a spoken response of short prayers of praise. Finish by saying (or even singing!) the Doxology together.

Praise God from whom all blessings flow.
Praise him all creatures here below.
Praise him above, ye heavenly host.
Praise Father, Son and Holy Ghost.

Note

Other choices for words could be a psalm or triumphant Easter hymn. The poem 'Easter Hymn' by Henry Vaughan, or even the more contemporary 'When there was nothing' by Stuart Henderson could also be suitable.

(79) SEEING IS BELIEVING

This exercise introduces a way of engaging with Scripture through the senses and the imagination which was practised by Ignatius of Loyola. By guiding the group in this way, you may well open up the Ignatian method for people to continue to explore fruitfully on their own.

You will need your Bible reading, and a simple prepared meditation script. The passages that are particularly effective are those involving an interaction with Jesus. The Gospels of Mark and Luke are good sources, though the following exercise is drawn from John.

Explain that we will use a method of Bible-based praying practised by St Ignatius of Loyola. We seek to live through a Bible passage by entering into the scene using our senses and imagination to bring it to life. By engaging with the story in this way we find ourselves meeting the Jesus of the Scriptures, who is alive here and now.

Some people find using their imagination easier than others. Encourage people to take part in the exercise as they can. The important thing is to be open to encountering Jesus.

Read John 20.19–23. This sets the scene, but we are going to put ourselves in the place of the disciple not there on that occasion: Thomas. Read verses 24–29.

Encourage people to settle into a relaxed but attentive position, and be open to meet the Lord through his Word.

The prayer leader guides the meditation

... You're walking towards the house where you'll meet up with the other disciples again ... You weren't with them last week, but they told you all about it, in fact they wouldn't stop talking about it ... They said they saw the Lord, just two days after he'd been crucified ... You said you'd need to touch Jesus' nail-marks and wounded side yourself before you'd believe that ... You reflect on what made you say that ... how it felt to have been absent the night this was supposed to have happened ... and how you feel about the disciples you're about to see in that very room now a whole week has gone by ... You walk up the street to that familiar house ... What does it look like? ... How do you feel as you approach it? ... Step inside the main door and be aware of the change in the air and light as you come in from the outside ... You hear the voices of your fellow disciples ... Make your way to where they are ... What do you see? ... Have all the others arrived? ... Can you see Peter ... James ... John ... Andrew? ... What are they doing? As you gather, you reflect on the fact that Judas won't be joining you ... How do you feel about that? ... What is it like to meet the disciples again here? ... Someone suggests shutting the door ... Who goes and does this? ... Be aware of any change of atmosphere as the door is closed ... Continue to be with the group, aware of everyone's mood, body language, conversation ...

And now – Jesus is in the room! ... Note the impact of suddenly discovering him among you ... What's happening as he comes and stands among you all? . . . What does he look like to you? . . . This is what the others said happened last week when you weren't here . . . How does it feel that it's actually happening again now you're here? . . . You become aware of how Jesus' coming in has changed things around you . . . of how the others are reacting and interacting with Jesus . . . Now be aware of how *you're* reacting, and what you choose to do . . . How do you feel about Jesus' being here? . . . He speaks: 'Peace be with you' . . . Note your response to these words . . . And be aware of your own body language, thoughts and feelings towards him . . . Now you become aware that Jesus is turning towards you and looking directly at you . . . How does it feel to be in his gaze? . . . He calls your name . . . What happens inside you as he does that? . . . Everyone's attention is now fully on you . . . Now Jesus' is inviting you to trace the nail-marks in his hands, and feel his side . . . You realize he knows exactly what you've been saying about him . . . How does that make you feel? . . . Decide how you will respond to his invitation . . . What is Jesus doing? . . . You want to acknowledge Jesus as 'my Lord and my God'. How do you say these words to him, and what is your body language as you speak them out? . . . Now you have spoken them, how does Jesus respond? . . . You hear Jesus bless those who have not 'seen' as you do and yet have come to believe . . . How does that make you feel? . . . Continue to focus on Jesus . . . Is there anything more you want to say to him? . . . Do you hear him say anything more to you personally? . . .

Now you become aware that Jesus is leaving . . . Watch him depart . . . What do you and the other disciples do now he is gone? . . . Reflect on what has changed for you as a result of this encounter with the risen Lord . . . And in your own time, come back into this room, at this time.

Invite the group to share how they found this exercise, as people can have quite different experiences of the same passage. It can be particularly interesting to discuss how they have pictured Jesus.

10

Pentecost and Trinity

Jesus promised that, after his Ascension, power would come from on high in the form of the Holy Spirit. At Pentecost we celebrate the fulfilment of that promise to all believers. The prayer themes of Pentecost centre on the freedom that the Spirit brings, and areas where his release and deliverance are still needed.

In our praises we thank God for his faithfulness in sending his Spirit upon his people. We intercede that the one Holy Spirit might bring unity among Christians. We pray with energy and urgency for the Church's mission, that the Holy Spirit will empower the proclaiming of the Good News to all nations. In our personal prayers we seek to be open to the Spirit's gifts, that he might equip us to serve the Lord where he wills. We ask that the Holy Spirit might work in us day by day, forming the fruit of Christ's character in our lives.

While the world around us relies on its own resources to solve problems and provide power for living, we look beyond ourselves to our life-bringing God, who gives generously to those who will submit themselves to him.

(80) TO ALL NATIONS

You will need to copy the same Bible verse in different languages, including English, on to separate pieces of paper. These should represent countries across the whole world, and preferably include some that use different scripts. (You can find John 3.16 in various languages on the website <www.tracts.com>, in the Seeds Tracts section. The Lord's Prayer in different languages can be found on the <www.christusrex.org> site, on the Convent of the Pater Noster page.)

You will also need a copy of the national flag of each language represented, on separate pieces of paper. Use a flag of a different English-speaking nation for the Bible verse in English. Put a number on each copy of the Bible verse, and a letter on each of the flags.

Arrange the Bible verses and flags randomly on a table in the middle of the group. Divide the group into two teams and give each a piece of paper and pen. Ask them to match each Bible verse to its appropriate flag. Once the teams have completed this task, give out the answers and establish the winner.

Now read the account of Pentecost in Acts 2.1–21. Explain that the languages heard here represented people from across the known world at that time ('from every nation under heaven', v. 5). Now the gospel is being spread ever more widely through languages spoken across the whole span of the globe.

The competing teams now co-operate in prayer. A team member from the winning team offers a short prayer for one of the countries represented by the flags and verses. A member of the other team then prays for another of the nations, and so on until all have been prayed for. Then both teams unite by declaring together the Bible verse written in English to complete the prayer time.

Note

You might prefer to do the matching part of this activity in smaller teams of twos or threes, or alternatively as a full group discussion. You could also swap the flags for a large map of the world, and locate the languages by placing the verses next to the nations they represent.

(81) FOR EVERY OCCASION

As Spirit-filled Christians, we are urged by Paul to 'pray without ceasing' and 'give thanks in all circumstances'.* Celtic Christians took this seriously by praying throughout the day over the ordinary tasks of life, from churning butter to lighting a fire. The next exercise seeks to update that practice.

You will need pens, small sheets of paper and a bowl.

Ask group members to write down some ordinary task that forms part of their everyday life (e.g. driving a car, washing up, working a photocopier, etc.), then to fold up their paper and put it into the bowl.

Next, pass the bowl round, asking each person to take out a piece of paper and look at the task written on it. They are to think of and write down a short prayer that could be said while doing this task – a prayer of thanksgiving, reflective prayer or intercession inspired by what the task suggests. Encourage people to use their creative spiritual imagination!

Once this been done, ask people to read their prayers out in turn as an act of worship.

Encourage group members to take away the prayer linked to their particular task, and use it throughout the following week.

* 1 Thessalonians 5.17, 18

You may wish to ask for feedback when the group next meets. Did they use their prayer? Has it made a difference to their experience of Christ in all aspects of life?

(82) SPIRITUAL FRUIT

You will need a piece of paper, on which you have written the fruit of the Spirit, as listed in Galatians 5.22, large enough for all to see and read clearly.

You will also need a plate of pieces of a segmented fruit, such as an orange. A bunch of grapes could be used as an alternative.

Place the list of the fruit of the Spirit in the middle of the group. Explain that in our prayers we're responding to Paul's call for Christians to 'live by the Spirit' (Galatians 5.16), showing the fruit of Christ-likeness as we allow his Spirit to be at work in us day by day. Invite group members to settle down into quiet attentiveness, ready to listen for the Spirit underlining which particular fruit he wants to grow in their lives at this time.

Open the prayer time by reading out the list slowly. To encourage a reflective focus, you may wish to amplify each fruit with a brief definition, along the lines suggested below:

Love:	the heart to act for the well-being and best interest of another
Joy:	the deep, underlying rejoicing that all things shall be well
Peace:	the inner harmony that radiates outward in a reconciling touch
Patience:	the ability to wait for God's time without forcing the pace

Kindness: the personal attention that lets others know they are cherished

Goodness: the gold of integrity that makes a person beautiful on the inside

Faithfulness: the gift of unwavering loyalty regardless of reward

Gentleness: the strength subdued under a discipline that protects and respects

Self-control: the poise not pressurized by the temptation to indulge self

Once the list is read and you've allowed some moments for personal reflection, the plate of fruit is passed round. Each person offers his or her neighbour an orange segment, along with the prayer: '**May the Spirit cause his fruit to grow in your life.**'

Encourage the one receiving the fruit to eat and savour it as a symbol of taking in the Spirit's nourishment to bring God's growth within.

Dependent on the group, people may wish to share afterwards in twos or threes which fruit they asked for.

(83) THE WIND OF THE SPIRIT

You will need a directional electric fan with at least two settings. This should be placed at the front of the group, and set up so people can come forward and position themselves in its path.

While you may wish to use some appropriate music, the sound of the fan itself provides a powerful backdrop to this prayer activity.

Explain that when the Holy Spirit descended on the disciples praying together at Pentecost, there was a noise of rushing

143

wind (described in Acts 2.1, 2). As another praying group of believers, we can express our openness to the Spirit coming upon us in the same way.

Open the prayer time by reading John 3:8:

'The wind blows where it chooses, and you hear the sound of it, but you do not know where it comes from or where it goes. So it is with everyone who is born of the Spirit.'

Turn the fan on to a low setting. Encourage people to quieten themselves and tune into the fan's whirr as a way of focusing attention and letting go of other concerns. (*Pause*)

The Spirit can come as a gentle breeze:
a breeze that enlivens us where we've become weary;
a breeze that cools us where we're overheated;
a breeze that calms us where we're overwrought;
a breeze that refreshes what has become stale.
Do we long for this breath of fresh air?

Ask people to let the Spirit prompt an awareness of aspects of their lives where his gentle breeze needs to breathe into them. Invite people in their own time to come and stand/sit for a few moments in the fan's path, as their personal prayer of receiving the breeze of the Spirit.

Now turn the fan up to a high setting. (*Pause*)

The Spirit can come as a mighty wind:
a wind that energizes us where we've become inactive;
a wind that stirs up what is buried deep inside;
a wind that carries us along and speeds our course;
a wind that blows over our structures and defences that
    keep God at a safe distance.
Are we willing to welcome this wind?

Ask people to let the Spirit bring to attention aspects of their lives where his powerful wind wants to blow. Invite them in their own time to come and stand/sit for some moments in the fan's path as their personal prayer of welcoming the wind of the Spirit.

Now turn the fan off. After all the wind's activity, there is stillness. Allow some moments for people to hear what God might be saying to them in the silence. (*Pause*)

Close with a prayer, thanking God for the gift and activity of his Spirit, and asking him to continue to work in everyone's lives as he chooses.

Note

The twelfth-century mystic Hildegard of Bingen described herself as a 'feather on the breath of God'. You may wish to use her words as a basis for an alternative activity. Give each person a feather and invite them one by one to release their feather into the fan's breeze as a prayer of willingness for God to blow through them by his Spirit, and send them wherever he lovingly chooses for his purposes.

(84) HAPPY BIRTHDAY TO YOU

You will need pieces of different coloured card, cut and folded to make blank greeting cards. You will also need felt-tip pens, plus any other card-making materials you wish to include, such as glitter, glue, tissue paper, gold and silver pens, inks and stamp pads, sequins, stars, etc.

You may wish to have some sample birthday cards to hand.

Conclude the prayer exercise with refreshments, including a cake as a 'birthday cake' for the Church. A fruit cake is a good choice as it illustrates how individuals expressing the fruit of the Spirit combine to offer nourishment to a needy world – though you may prefer to draw on the symbolic potential of a well-risen sponge!

Explain that as Pentecost is often seen as the birthday of the Christian Church, our prayer activity will celebrate the occasion.

Ask people to work in pairs, and make a birthday card to 'send' to the Church. They are to create the picture or design on the front, and inside the card write a message to the Church. They also need to include a P.S. that lets the Church know that a present is on its way, and to indicate what this present is to be. As the Spirit who came at Pentecost gifted the Apostles – most immediately with the gift of other languages – so each pair is to think what present they would most like to send to bless and equip the Church today.

Once the cards are completed, ask each pair in turn to stand theirs on the table, read the message and say what gift they are sending to the Church and why.

With the cards now on display, have a prayer time where you praise and thank God for the Church's birthday, and pray for the Church along the lines suggested by the gift ideas. Ask that God by his Spirit will indeed give the Church what she needs at this time.

After you have prayed together, cut the Church's 'birthday cake' and enjoy food and fellowship in an impromptu birthday party.

Note

If you want to maintain a celebratory emphasis, you could focus your prayer time on thanksgiving with **Party Popper Prayers.** Give each person a party popper, which they pull as they offer a prayer of thanksgiving for some aspect of the Church.

(85) TRINITY TRIANGLES

You will need a set of triangles cut from card of different colours, plus writing materials. The triangles need to be of the same size, as the prayer activity involves piecing them together to form one larger triangle. If the number of group members does not tally with an exact number of small triangles needed to form the larger one, you will need to prepare some extra triangles on which you have either composed or copied other Trinity prayers. Celtic prayer books are a good source for these, as they have a strong Trinitarian emphasis. The concluding prayer suggested here is taken from the Carmina Gadelica *(a collection of songs, prayers and blessings from the oral tradition of Scotland and the Western Highlands).*

Explain how as Christians we worship the threefold God who is Father, Son and Holy Spirit. Explore together what aspects of God we associate with the different persons of the Trinity: the Father who is the Creator and Sustainer of all; the Son who has become one of us, our Redeemer and Saviour; the Spirit who is the life of God sent forth upon us, bringing God's gifts, power, comfort and guidance.

Give everyone a card triangle, and ask them to write on it a three-line prayer of praise or thanksgiving to each person of the Trinity – one line per person. People may wish to write their prayer along their triangle's three sides.

Allow some time for this, and, when all have finished, open the prayer time. Invite each person going round the group in turn to read out his or her prayer and place the triangle on the table. As one after another adds in a triangle, people need to be aware that they're contributing to making a larger triangle. If you have needed to supplement the group's triangles with some extras, distribute these and ask those receiving them to pray the prayer on their card and add it to the table to complete the shape.

Once the triangle is made, spend a few moments reflecting on the kaleidoscope of combined colours and prayers displayed. Finish by reading a Trinitarian blessing prayer, such as:

Be the eye of God dwelling with you,
the foot of Christ in guidance with you,
the shower of the Spirit pouring on you,
richly and generously.
Amen.

Further resources

The following suggestions are obviously personal and selective, but I hope they might provide a starting point for your own creative exploration of the resources around in words, music, images, visual aids and others' ideas. You may need to be prepared to do some adapting and adjusting. Most available material currently tends to be *either* for a large congregational setting, *or* for the individual, rather than the small informal group in between.

Prayers and poems

The Christian Church never seems short of words. We study the Word of God to encounter Jesus, the Living Word, and words, set or spontaneous, form the currency of our communication in corporate worship.

While spontaneous spoken prayers are sometimes viewed as more spiritual and sincere, praying in groups is enhanced rather than diminished by incorporating set, written words. Encouraging group members to write their own prayers can give them space to clarify what they want to say to God. Prayers written by others can also be helpful: we recognize our own experience as others' words encapsulate and crystallize thoughts and feelings we've not previously been able to bring out of ourselves to offer to God.

Coleridge described poetry as 'the best words in the best order'. The Psalms themselves are poems, and can help us voice to God what we'd sometimes like to say but do not dare. Religious poetry can be a powerful stimulus for meditative prayer. People do not need to struggle to understand every line as it is read, but can stay with particular phrases, or allow the sound of the words to wash over them in God's presence.

You could invite the group to choose a prayer meaningful for them, or read aloud a poem or prayer for reflection or to lead into spoken response. If you intend to accompany your words with background music, test out your material with possible music choices beforehand. You'll quickly gauge which piece 'fits' best. A group member less confident with extempore prayer may feel able to lead such worship.

Simple liturgies and short set responses spoken together can unite the group, enabling all to pray out loud together. Instead of looking for other resources, your and your group could create your own prayer responses. In writing these, aim to be crisp and direct in style and construction, and avoid the temptation of overcomplicated sentences and flowery language.

Prayer collections

David Adam (ed.), *A Celtic Psaltery*. SPCK 2001.

Angela Ashwin (ed.), *The Book of a Thousand Prayers*. Zondervan 2002.

Mary Batchelor (ed.), *The Lion Prayer Collection*. Lion 2001.

Geoffrey Duncan (ed.), *A Lifetime of Blessing*. Canterbury Press 2004.

Robin Keeley (ed.), *Prayers Encircling the World*. SPCK 1998.

The SPCK Book of Christian Prayer. SPCK 1995.

Poetry and reflective books

*Liz Babbs (music: Simeon Wood), *The Celtic Heart*. Lion 2004.

John Henstridge, *Transforming the Ordinary*. BRF 2004.

Anthony de Mello, *Sadhana: A Way to God*. Doubleday Image 1984.

Peter Millar. *Surprise of the Sacred*. Canterbury Press 2004.

Philip Newell, *Earthful of Glory*. SPCK 1996.

Joyce Rupp, *Out of the Ordinary: Prayers, poems and reflections for every season*. Ave Maria Press 2000.

Andrea Skevington (ed.), *Poems to Get You Through the Week*. Lion 2004.

*Jean Watson (ed.), *The Spirit of Tranquillity*. Lion 2004.

David Winter (ed.), *The Poets' Christ*. Lion 1998.

*Both with accompanying music CD.

Liturgical material

Dorothy McRae-McMahon, *Prayers for Life's Particular Moments*. SPCK 2001.

Janet Morley, *All Desires Known*. SPCK 2005.

Northumbria Community, *Celtic Daily Prayer*. HarperCollins 2000.

Ray Simpson, *Prayer Rhythms: The Celtic Prayer Book Vol. 1*. Kevin Mayhew 2003.

Wild Goose Worship Group, *A Wee Worship Book*. Wild Goose Publications 1999.

Eldred Willey (ed.), *First Light*. Darton, Longman & Todd 2001.

Melodies and moods

Martin Luther described music as 'one of the most magnificent and delightful presents God has given us', and used sensitively and appropriately it's a gift that can powerfully enhance a group's prayer life.

In selecting music, think carefully about its place and purpose in your prayer time. Do you want people to listen to the music as a specific focus, or is it there to provide an accompaniment to a prayer activity or spoken words? Will you use instrumental or vocal music? If the latter, you need to consider whether the words will emphasize the direction of the prayers or become a distraction.

Consider what mood or impact you want your music to create. This can range from reflective and calming for meditative prayer, to uplifting and energizing for the praise of a jubilant psalm, and many other possibilities in between.

Decide whether music will play throughout your prayer activity or just for a particular part of it. You may simply wish to 'top and tail' a meditative exercise with some appropriate music to lead people gently into and out of prayer.

Will you opt for music that is classical or more contemporary, sacred or secular? It's also worth considering whether your chosen music has any prominent associations with a current film or advertising campaign, if you want it to do the job for which *you* intend it! However, associations can be exploited positively: an instrumental version of a well-known Christian hymn or song will provide the flavour of the original without the immediate distraction of the actual words.

Remember that it's not always a 'must' to have the CD player on: there's also the music of sheer silence.

Reflective music CDs

Agnus Dei from Classical Music and Meditation series. Naxos 1999.

Calm from Body and Soul series. (Also *Sunday Morning.*) Union Square Music 2000.

Chillout Worship for Meditation and Worship. Authentic Music 2003 and 2004.

Favourite Gregorian Chant. Classics for Pleasure. EMI 1994.

Instrumental Worship series 1–6. Kingsway Music 2003 and 2004.

Officium. Jan Garbarek and the Hilliard Ensemble. ECM 1994.

Perfect Time. Maire Brennan. Word Records 1998.

Vaughan Williams and Delius. Essential Classics. Sony Music 2001 (especially 'The Lark Ascending' – Vaughan Williams; 'In a Summer Garden' – Delius).

The Very Best of Relaxing Classics. Decca 2003 (especially 'Canon in D' – Pachelbel; 'Gymnopédie' 1 – Erik Satie; 'Morning Suite' from *Peer Gynt* – Grieg; 'Cavatina' – Stanley Myers; the John Dunbar theme from *Dances with Wolves* – John Barry).

Vivaldi: Four Seasons. Unforgettable Classics. EMI 1995.

Your Favourite Taizé Collection. Alliance Music 2000.

Sounds of nature

Some CDs interweave natural sounds with music, though this is not the case with those suggested below.

Monastery Garden. New World Company 1994.

Ocean Surf. Music Collection International Ltd 1997.

Wilderness River. Echoes of Nature. Delta Music GmbH 1995.

Participative music

Taizé Songs for Prayer. Decani Music 1998 (also see <www.taize.fr>).

A Wee Worship Book. Wild Goose Worship Group. Wild Goose Publications 1999.

Signs and symbols

Jesus brought people into a deeper awareness of his unseen spiritual Kingdom by using familiar aspects of the physical world around him, in his parables and through his actions. Most supremely, he instituted the Eucharist, where we meet him in the common elements of bread and wine.

As we look for signs and symbols to earth our prayers and make real the heavenly connection in our day, we can ask for Jesus' eyes to see the spiritual potential of what lies around us.

Start your search by reading the Bible passage relevant for your group meeting, and let your imagination roam free as you reflect on what prayer it inspires in you in response, and what aspect of day-to-day living you might use to express this.

Seek to stay in tune spiritually throughout the day. As you use everyday items and engage in ordinary activities – from getting dressed to using the TV remote control – be open to what parallels they might have with the Christian life. Can they be linked into a prayer communication in some way?

Actively set aside time to go on a prayer-expedition to hunt for creative ideas and resources beyond your own home.

Saunter through your local market and browse around the stalls: look, listen, touch, smell and taste – and seek to be receptive to the links the Holy Spirit might prompt.

Visit your local supermarket, DIY or general store. What bits and pieces on sale could be adapted for a prayerful purpose? Drop into your nearest garden centre for inspiration from the plants and paraphernalia. Craft shops also have a wealth of small items that can form useful resources for creative prayer connections.

Walk out into natural surroundings such as a garden, park or woods. You might find objects you could bring back and use.

Wherever you go shopping or exploring, it's worth keeping your eye open for those two most valuable resources: stones and candles. Both come in all shapes and sizes, and could inspire you in many prayer activities beyond the suggestions in this book.

Stones range from tiny pebbles to large rocks. They may be rough or smooth, plain or decorated. (Some retreat houses have stones inscribed with Celtic Christian motifs.) Coloured glass nuggets have become very popular and also have creative prayer potential. Be aware, too, of the wide variety of candles and holders around. How could you use floating candles,

candles with three wicks, and tea-lights of different colours and fragrances, rather than just plain white?

However, as with all creative praying, don't feel you have to devise something clever and complicated. Often the simplest ideas are the most effective and memorable.

Pictures and pointers

It's said that a picture is worth a thousand words, which makes it an immediate and profound medium of communication, not least in prayer. Several activities suggested in this book involve the person praying in creating a drawing, but we can also use pictures and images to receive communication from God (see suggestion 55). These become windows through which we see what God chooses to reveal about himself and our relationship with him.

As with music, the picture forming the focus of your prayer time needs to be chosen with prayer: painting or photograph? Representational or more abstract? Will the subject matter be overtly sacred, or broadly secular? A work of art does not have to be of specifically religious intent in order for God to speak through it. It need not even be a pretty sight, but bear in mind the sensitivity and age-range of your group if you want to choose more challenging material. The 'Philippians test' applies: 'Whatever is true, whatever is honourable, whatever is just, whatever is pure, whatever is pleasing, whatever is commendable, if there is any excellence and if there is anything worthy of praise, think on these things' (Philippians 4.8, 9).

If there is no suitable painting, poster or calendar scene readily accessible, you could search for an image on the internet to display on a computer screen. (Depending on your time and creative technological skills, a PowerPoint sequence of images with music or words can be a stimulus for reflection or praise.)

You may also have pieces of sculpture or other God-created or man-made artistic objects around your home that could be used to great effect.

Visual resource material

John Drury, *Painting the Word: Christian Pictures and their Meanings.* Yale University Press 2002.

Craig Brian Larson and Lori Quicke, *Movie-Based Illustrations for Preaching and Teaching: 101 Clips to Show and Tell.* Zondervan 2003.

Kenneth Lawrence (ed.), J. Weaver and R. Wedell, *Imaging the Word: An Arts and Lectionary Resource Vol. 1.* United Church Press 1994.

Words and websites

As you develop your experience in creative praying, you may wish to draw on the insights of others. The suggestions below cover explorations of the various aspects of creative praying, as well as providing further resources and ideas. While some are oriented towards individual praying, they may trigger thoughts of an approach you could try in a group situation. You will find most 'hands-on' prayer activities under the heading of children's worship ideas, but that does not mean that they cannot be used by those of all ages.

Books to engage and inspire

Jeffrey Arnold, *The Big Book on Small Groups.* IVP 1992 (includes sections on worship and prayer in a group setting).

Jonny Baker and Doug Gay with Jenny Brown, *Alternative Worship.* SPCK 2003.

Bruce Duncan, *Pray Your Way.* Darton, Longman & Todd 1993.

Ruth Fowke and Pam Dobson, *Creativity and Prayer*. Eagle 1998.

Peter Graystone and Eileen Turner, *A Church for All Ages*. Scripture Union 1993 (section on creative acts of worship).

Sheila Pritchard, *The Lost Art of Meditation*. Scripture Union 2003.

Margaret Silf, *Taste and See: Adventuring into Prayer*. Darton, Longman & Todd 1999.

Sue Wallace, *Multi-Sensory Prayer*. Scripture Union 2000.

Some websites with prayer ideas

www.alternativeworship.org
www.brf.org.uk/barnabas
www.portsmouth.anglican.org/spirituality
www.prayerwindows.com
www.prayerrequests.co.uk
www.salvationarmy.org.uk/alove ('Engage' page)

Index of Bible references

Index of Bible references

159

Index of themes

Index of themes

Index of themes

The Society for Promoting Christian Knowledge (SPCK) was founded in 1698. Its mission statement is:

To promote Christian knowledge by

- **Communicating the Christian faith in its rich diversity;**
- **Helping people to understand the Christian faith and to develop their personal faith; and**
- **Equipping Christians for mission and ministry.**

SPCK Worldwide serves the Church through Christian literature and communication projects in over 100 countries, and provides books for those training for ministry in many parts of the developing world. This worldwide service depends upon the generosity of others and all gifts are spent wholly on ministry programmes, without deductions.

SPCK Bookshops support the life of the Christian community by making available a full range of Christian literature and other resources, providing support for those training for ministry, and assisting bookstalls and book agents throughout the UK.

SPCK Publishing produces Christian books and resources, covering a wide range of inspirational, pastoral, practical and academic subjects. Authors are drawn from many different Christian traditions, and publications aim to meet the needs of a wide variety of readers in the UK and throughout the world.

The Society does not necessarily endorse the individual views contained in its publications, but hopes they stimulate readers to think about and further develop their Christian faith.

For further information about the Society, visit our website at *www.spck.org.uk* or write to:
SPCK, 36 Causton Street,
London SW1P 4ST, United Kingdom.